REFLECTIONS

ON

PSYCHOTHERAPY

AND

PATHS FOR WELLBEING

Veis Djalali, PhD

Veis Djalali

ISBN: 978-0-69243-476-5

Published by Wynnpix Productions
Cover design by Veis Djalali
Author photograph by Nahid Massoud
Cover layout by Webmark

I dedicate this book to the patients I have had the privilege to know and care about. Thank you for letting me share in your journeys.

క్రిక్రిక్రి

Veis Djalali

ଔଔଔଔଔଔଔ

Reflections on Psychotherapy

TABLE OF CONTENTS

INTRODUCTION

If you don't like something, change it.
If you can't change it, change your attitude.

—Maya Angelou

The value and success of psychotherapy, in terms of healing and change, has been explored and questioned in research as well as by the general public.

This book is a strong proponent of the belief that the opportunity to change and grow toward wellbeing and health is ever present and an option of choice. However, psychological "readiness" for positive growth is an individual process and often not within easy reach. Acquiring this "readiness" is where psychotherapy aspires to be most effective. It requires a great deal of courage, willingness, and motivation to risk leaving one's comfort zones and to undertake the adventure into unknown territory that can bring about a change in behavior and/or attitude.

Psychotherapy assesses the psychological "readiness" of a person who is unhappy with his or her life. It also evaluates the directions and choices that emerge which will provide the avenues for change and movement toward positive health and wellbeing.

❦X❦

Reflections on Psychotherapy

This book offers an anthology of case studies about patients who struggled to find ways to change their various situations throughout the course of their lifespan. The patients' narratives attest to the fact that change and growth can indeed be attained. Psychotherapy can be a powerful tool that helps in the process of building strength, opening doors to enlightenment, and creating understandings and self-discoveries.

Psychotherapy tends the wounded psyche and provides clients with the tools for healing. If the timing is well synchronized, the therapeutic experience can be extremely rewarding and reenergizing. The healing experience often generalizes to other aspects of the patient's personality and can last a lifetime.

In eighteen essays, this book describes the process of psychotherapy from the perspective of various issues. The essays also reflect the unique relationship that emerges between patient and psychotherapist. The essays have been written to stand independently. Each presents an issue, and then explores its psychodynamics. A case study is used to demonstrate and describe some patient's struggles with that particular issue. An analysis of the case follows subsequent to the presentation. These sample patients are drawn from a pool based on direct experience in clinical practice. The anonymity of the players in these case studies is strictly and sensitively observed.

In order to protect and fortify patient/therapist confidentiality, no particular person is revealed in his or her actuality. The case studies are composites of several patients and situations. They are designed to coincide with the psychology and dynamics of the issues being presented.

The aim of this book is to portray the narratives of those who seek psychotherapy, as well as to depict the work that psychotherapy entails. The psychotherapist's authenticity, care, and ability to be a positive role model are also emphasized. In the journey toward healing, being creative and resourceful is encouraged for both therapist and patient.

This book is designed to convey the flavor of psychotherapy, to provoke thought and questions, and to serve as a learning tool for students of clinical psychology.

෪෪෪෪

THE EFFECTIVE THERAPIST

Many people from various walks of life and theoretical backgrounds train to become psychotherapists. The characteristics that constitute effectiveness, however, are not necessarily found in theoretical modalities, monetary success, "scientific validations," or fame. What has become apparent is that certain states of being, of relating, and of connecting contribute most to the effectiveness of a therapist, and to the degree of positive impact they can have on their patients. These significant states of relating are described in this essay.

CRCRCR

Caring

The most effective characteristic of a successful psychotherapist is his or her humanity and inherent caring. This is a quality that can neither be learned nor acquired; it is either an integral part of a person's personality or it is not. Some therapists may lack good skills or broad wisdom and knowledge, but they have this essential empathy and caring. Others might be extremely skillful and learned, but lack compassion and caring. It is when both caring and skill exist together and are expressed by the psychotherapist that effectiveness has its highest impact. True caring, or the lack thereof, is always meta-communicated from psychotherapist to patient. The ways in which those exchanges are employed and received, abused, rejected, or manipulated become part of the therapeutic process and central to the art of psychotherapy.

ରୀରୀରୀ

Listening

The ability to listen well is another major aspect of psychotherapeutic effectiveness. How to listen well is something that can be taught in training. The therapist's initial caring, however, is what motivates and guides the ability to listen effectively. Listening, as used in the art of psychotherapy, is not a simple skill. There are many layers to effective listening; it encompasses a vast and complex territory in communication.

Listening involves hearing what is said *and* what is omitted. There is always content, but this content is often not the intent of the communication. In fact, intentions can be obscure and even unrealized by the person who is speaking. Sometimes intentions are known and deliberately hidden. Other times, intentions are realized in the process of communication and can change even as the message is delivered. It is crucial to develop the ability to decipher the intentions of a message, and not just hear the words delivered. To understand any communication fully also involves being aware of the larger context of the relationship between speaker and listener. A communicator's delivery, attitude, demeanor, vocal tone, and body language all play a role in the message's meaning, and must be absorbed by the artful listener.

The psychotherapist is listening not only to the patient, but also, simultaneously, to his or her own intuition, and incorporating learned skills and acquired knowledge, along with the ability to be objective and hold a wider perspective. At the same instant, in the interactions between patient and therapist, there is a relationship brewing that also becomes part of the therapeutic process and has its own nuances.

So, as the patient relates a story, the psychotherapist listens to the content of the story as it is told in the moment. The psychotherapist also actively views all aspects of the patient and the ways in which the story is being told and not told. The psychotherapist needs to have good self-awareness and be in touch with his or her own intuitive responses, always maintaining a distinct understanding of the boundaries between himself or herself, as a separate subject from the patient. And the psychotherapist is ever cognizant of the emerging and evolving relationship between patient and therapist, with all of its implications.

This kind of listening is very organic; it involves the entire being of the therapist in a fully present and creative sense. It requires close attentiveness to the self, to the other, and to the interaction between the two. It also requires an objective awareness of the three processes operating simultaneously and the responsibility to act accordingly.

In this respect, psychotherapy can be viewed as *an art form.*

Not all psychotherapists who are considered to be effective practice their craft as an art form. Notions of effectiveness vary and can be argued. But for those who do view psychotherapy more as an art than strictly as a science, a path emerges that is uniquely creative, one that requires an uninhibited but secure flow of observations and reactions.

For a therapist to have confidence in his or her spontaneous expressions and to tap their unique creativity, they need a strong and healthy foundation in themselves. That is a prerequisite for this type of communication.

A healthy security within the psychotherapist's sense of self allows them to operate in the present and to be mindful at the same time. The familiar defenses that are required outside of the therapeutic space are not admitted into these authentic interactions. An open, immediate presence and a non-defensive posture prohibit responses from being muddled and/or from confusing the creative therapist's listening and close attentiveness. This is an authentic, liberating, and ethical mode of caring and connecting to another human being, one that invites healing and responsible self-awareness.

ෆ෨෨෨

Timing

As discussed above, listening is complex. The artful psychotherapist develops an acute sense of timing, starting with an evaluation of each patient's "readiness." Effective intervention involves knowing the therapeutic value of when to interrupt, when to interact, when to self-disclose, and when to just be quiet. Often, psychotherapists offer pearls of wisdom, suggestions and advice that land on deaf ears. If the therapist is overly invested in what they offer and suggest, or if the communication is ill-timed, then the relationship between therapist and patient can be marred by the psychotherapist's ego.

Those who seek therapy have their own timing in terms of when they can best hear and receive guidance and then act on resolutions. The most effective practice for the therapist is to devise situations that will impact their client's own quest and stage of learning. Patients have their own individual pace for coming to know and understand the meaning of their behaviors and conflicts in relationships and events. The only benefit in giving answers and solutions prematurely is that it tests the client's timing process and draws attention to the areas where the patient is not "ready" for intervention. Depending on the impact of the solution given and the ensuing results, the therapist can then backtrack and continue with the chipping-away process at the client's preferred pace.

When clients are guided to discover their own answers, their resolve has much more meaning and greater depth. It can sometimes be difficult for the psychotherapist to hang back and proceed at the client's pace, especially when the answer is so obvious and clear to them. Great patience, motivated by the knowledge of what is most effective, is required to lend support to the psychotherapist's dilemma.

଼ଣଣଣ

The Interactive Process

Those in therapy have often vocalized their displeasure about therapists who present themselves as a blank canvas and limit their interactions to a minimum. The purpose of this style of conducting therapy is to give full rein to the patient while not interfering in the disclosures through the use of prompts.

For the artful therapist, however, it can be effective and useful to share reactions, to give feedback, and to interact with patients. Interactions between client and therapist can enhance their relationship; they can also give the therapist firsthand knowledge of their client's methods of relating. These interactions need to be within the context of the therapy and intended solely to benefit the therapeutic process. They are not supposed to stroke the ego of the therapist or satisfy his or her needs. Again, the concept of *timing* is crucial.

Self-disclosures by the therapist can be useful at times, notably when they express the psychotherapist's fallibility and humanness. The therapist's role of guide and counselor can be enhanced, sometimes, by their not appearing to be superhuman and/or perfect. Other times, the therapist's life experiences can serve as concrete examples of some issue under scrutiny, thereby contributing to the client's understanding. It is also important to sit back and be quiet in order to allow a patient to struggle, emote, and recover without the therapist's active intervention. As discussed, the concepts of "timing," "listening" and "caring" are intertwined; all are necessary for effective psychotherapy.

∞∞∞

Attachment

The notion of attachment must be viewed differently by the effective psychotherapist. In expressing authenticity and caring in the therapeutic space, becoming overly attached is a possibility for both therapist and patient. The effective psychotherapist masters the ability to allow herself/himself to be open and to care, yet to maintain objectivity.

The connection between therapist and patient is unique. It is extremely significant and close, yet it is not a friendship or love relationship. Both patient and therapist need to understand the limits and confines of the therapeutic space. The freedom to be authentic and therapeutic has within it the aspiration to transcend the boundaries of love and friendship. Outside the therapeutic space, expressions of love and friendship are loaded with self-interest and personal needs. Inside the therapeutic space, however, the therapist studies his or her client's interests and needs in order to resolve conflicts and enhance self-awareness.

To be therapeutic is not entirely selfless: the psychotherapist is *motivated* to do good work and be effective. The personal needs of the therapist cannot interfere with the needs of the client, however. If those needs do get mixed with the patient's, the therapist's ability to "listen" and be fully "present" will be compromised. When over-attachment occurs for the therapist, their work's objectivity suffers. The result is that the therapist then needs to be liked and appreciated by her/his patient, and this need is meta-communicated to the patient; this will lead to a loss of both respect and the opportunity to be effective.

Often the over-attached therapist does not even realize the progress of his or her patient and the appropriate time to terminate their sessions together. Therapists with abandonment issues have a hard time letting go of their patients. Over-involvement may compromise a patient's growth toward health, autonomy, and wellbeing. The therapist's need to keep their relationship with the patient intact and ongoing can overwhelm the process and diminish their ability to be effective.

When a patient exhibits over-attachment toward their therapist, it is usually symptomatic of how they "normally" respond to a "love object." This "transference" has been written about in detail from a variety of therapeutic modalities. It is generally regarded as a *breakthrough phenomenon*, since it provides a good deal of substance for the therapeutic work. The dynamic demonstrates firsthand the nuances, expectations, worries, conflicts, and disappointments through the ways that the patient behaves when attached and in want. These occurrences have powerful implications and therapeutic potential. The material generated is essential for guiding the patient toward health as it helps to illuminate clearer understandings and leads to forming constructive behaviors.

For the effective psychotherapist, attachment becomes a balancing act: the goal is to be close, caring, and fully present, yet to remain objective in order to oversee the therapeutic dynamics.

For the patient, attachment to the therapist reveals the work that she or he needs to do, the guidance that is appropriate, and the behaviors that may need to be overcome.

ೱೢೱೢೱ

Monetary Gain

Dichotomies arise in this profession when monetary gain is included in the list of exchanges between therapist and client. Many patients are affronted by having to pay a therapist. In their opinion, listening to problems is not considered "work." For some, the act of payment is accompanied by cynical beliefs; they question the motives and authenticity of the paid therapist's pure devotion. Reconciling the therapist's care with monetary compensation can become a significant part of the therapeutic relationship.

Also, the therapist's scruples play a role. Some psychotherapists find it difficult to attach monetary value to their work, especially in the early years of training. Other psychotherapists feel very deserving, and have no conflicts in this regard. Perhaps, in an ideal world, all services like education, medicine, and legal needs should be socialized and freely available to the public. As it stands, however, the business aspect of this profession adds complexity to the mix.

The artful therapist should assess the client's relationship to the exchange of money and its subjective meanings, and then incorporate it into the work. Caring, in the authentic sense, cannot be fabricated. It is self-evident and meta-communicated, regardless of the business aspects of the relationship. Buying and selling are realities of life on many levels. It is honest to be upfront and clear about what is being offered and what is being accepted. This exchange supports and highlights the balance between the personal and objective parts of relationships.

A built-in advantage of exchanges that involve payment for service is the *power that the patient holds* in the relationship. In essence, the patient is the boss and the therapist is the employee. This reality dictates that the patient determines when to attend sessions or not, and when to terminate the relationship. The therapist's effectiveness is based on the patient's attendance and compliance. This reality check is a pragmatic factor that can mitigate the effects of attachment between therapist and client.

Sometimes patients may not be aware of their power in the therapeutic relationship. Patients may see themselves as weak and dependent on the therapist, assuming that the therapist is in charge or in control of the situation. When this is experienced, the power dynamic of should be clarified. The effective psychotherapist should position himself or herself merely as a guide who is employed by the patient to discover therapeutic paths. The therapist can aid the patient to see themselves as the party in control, with the ultimate choice of paying for a desired service.

In fact, it is the psychotherapist who is more at risk of becoming overly dependent in this relationship. The effective psychotherapist also wisely diversifies his/her sources of livelihood so as to not rely completely on the income generated by therapeutic encounters.

ಐಐಐಐ

Deceptions

Many people seem to credit psychologists with the power to see inside the heads of those with whom they come into contact. There is a popular, if erroneous, assumption that psychologists can detect falsehood to a higher degree than those not trained in the field. It cannot be stressed enough that *psychotherapists are fallible humans* and *can* be deceived just like anyone else. In fact, because of their training to be caring and attentive and to listen without judgment, psychotherapists are quite likely to be fooled by someone whose intentions are to mask themselves and play-act a falsehood.

In "listening" well, a psychotherapist will indeed pick up on inconsistencies between affect and what is being said. He or she may feel intuitively uneasy about a person, as well. These are clues to be pursued and explored, not judged. Therapy is a kind of detective work; its objective, however, is not to discover and condemn criminals.

Therapy's objectives are to understand the struggles of those in pain and to help expand horizons. The focus of forensic psychologists, on the other hand, is to decipher clues in order to aid the police in solving crimes and apprehending criminals.

The goals of an effective psychotherapist are to create the means by which a client can enhance self-awareness in order to better cope with conflicts. Her or his aim is to open the paths toward maturity, growth, and a coming to terms with human fallibilities. The effective psychotherapist is more adept at detecting pain than deceptions.

CROSCR

The Hazards of Being a Therapist

There are positive and negative consequences to any choice or way of being in the world. While there are many meaningful and fulfilling aspects to being a psychotherapist, there are also drawbacks. When working so intensely and authentically in the therapeutic space, it is at times difficult for a professional therapist to maintain equanimity in light of the superficiality that is so often encountered in the rest of life.

Life outside the therapeutic space is fraught with mundane busywork that requires very little presence of mind or full psychic participation. It is necessary to wear armor and maintain defenses when living in a world that does not offer the safety of the therapeutic space; the transition can be unpalatable.

For some therapists, switching gears from being enlivened to what feels like robotic behavior can offer them a respite from the therapeutic intensity, but still often feels distant and unfulfilling. On the other hand, there are psychotherapists who do not want to engage in any serious interactions outside of the therapy room. In their "down time," they seek out, at all costs, activities and types of play that do not bind them to a chair or put them in a listening position. They reserve the intensity and seriousness only for the therapy room. This kind of casual behavior can annoy those significant others in their personal relationships and cause difficulties for those who expect more attentive and closer connections.

Some people who are attracted to being in a relationship with a psychologist desire only a one-sided involvement, whether they are conscious of this desire or not. They want their therapist partner/friend to be of service to them and helpful when they need it; and they expect the therapist to have no needs or vulnerabilities of their own. When these, and other unrealistic expectations, are projected or assumed within these unbalanced relationships, and/or fail to be met, anger and disappointments invariably arise.

Other people believe that psychological training develops clairvoyance, and this can make them extremely self-consciousness around therapists, and hyper-vigilant about protecting their privacy. These people assume that the therapist "knows all" and "sees all," so, as a result, nothing needs to be said! Obviously, this is another kind of one-sided involvement that makes the natural course of relating and getting close very challenging.

From another perspective, those who are in a personal relationship with a psychologist may find that some of the very skills that are so valued in a therapy room are hard to bear in ordinary daily life. Being closely listened to and attended to can feel intrusive. The therapist's inability to small talk is yet another hindrance in daily interactions. Continuous, profound remarks made by the therapist in simple conversations may feel pedantic and superior. Meaningful intensity is not always appreciated or sought on all occasions or around all forms of social interaction.

Another hazard of being a psychologist is the internal clock that becomes a habitual way of relating to patients. When this extends to friends and family members, it can be irritating. Psychotherapeutic sessions are usually forty-five minutes to an hour in length. This time interval dictates the therapist's capacity for attentiveness and concentration. Once the hour is up, the therapist grows restless and needs a break to regroup. This internal clock works well in the therapy room but becomes inappropriate or negative when connecting with family and friends.

Psychotherapists are trained to break through barriers and shed patient defenses in safe, healing environments. In the "real world," however, having defenses is practical and appropriate. Defenses are developed as coping mechanisms for healthy survival. Learning to wear different hats as the situation demands is a useful and necessary lesson for the effective psychotherapist, both in their professional and personal lives.

಄಄಄

There are many other characteristics of the effective psychotherapist, but these are the basics.

಄಄಄

ESSENTIAL PREMISES

Psychotherapists operate from premises developed from their natural inclinations which are added to the knowledge that they acquire and the clinical experiences they garner. It is impossible to be free of premises. It is even more difficult to have conscious awareness of all the premises that guide a therapist's strategies and evaluations. However, it is wise for the psychotherapist to be as aware as possible of the premises that formulate his or her thinking, along with their effects on the works in progress. It is also prudent to keep an open mind and not be overly attached to these premises nor take them as gospels or inviolate truths.

This essay examines some of the significant premises that guide the ideology of this book and the treatments offered in the case studies.

ରେରେରେ

Mindsets

Most beliefs and values are formed in childhood. These beliefs are reshaped, modified, and reinforced through the progression of growth and other life experiences. It is the mind of a child, however, that stores realizations and understandings about life, and that forms subsequent attitudes toward the self and others. The blueprint for an individual's philosophies is formed in childhood. These beliefs become parts of an individual's personality, and they guide their future behaviors.

Change and redirection are always possible; but significant experiences have to take place in order for habitual thoughts to dislodge and for new formulations to come into effect. Any life event or realization can be life-changing and have significant impact on an individual's personality and attitudes.

The issues that most people explore in psychotherapy are the struggles of adults trying to come to terms with conflicts in their lives; their mindsets, however, were formulated and embedded in their psyche during childhood. A child's view is not equipped to handle adult concerns. The child's understandings, in fact, are set up for failure in the adult world. There are always strong tendencies to uphold these child-formed mindsets and to perpetuate them as reality. Even though these mindsets are no longer applicable, adults are inclined to hold on to what is familiar rather than to delve into unknown territory.

A good deal of the therapeutic intervention process is spent in the discovery and identification of these mindsets. The objective is to understand why the mindset was formed in the first place, and then to evaluate if it is still important, significant, or necessary to up hold for the wellbeing of the person in the present tense.

In fact, to attain health and wellbeing, it is crucial to rethink and develop more appropriate belief systems that suit the life and experiences of an adult. As people mature and grow along each developmental stage, their beliefs and attitudes also need to adapt and evolve. The original mindset of a child cannot foresee or understand the demands of the forthcoming stages; hence, children are not equipped to put adequate survival mechanisms in place.

ଜ୍ଜ୍ଜ

Expectations from Love

The expression and extension of love is often a primary concern for adults. How to love, what it means to be loved, what constitutes not being loved, and methods of how love is given and received are all learned and absorbed unconsciously during childhood. In couple's counseling, the meanings of love are often at the center of most disputes and misunderstandings. People have unconscious expectations from love. If love is not communicated in the manner that they expect, it is either not seen or rejected.

The art of loving occurs when an individual comprehends the particular meanings of love from the eyes and intentions of the other, without mixing in their own expectations. This is not an easy task, since the exchange is emotional and loaded with wounds sustained in the past. Most people want to be loved according to their own expectations. It is erroneously assumed that everyone's definition of love is the same. It is much easier to receive and feel the love that people have to offer once someone develops their own ability to understand the various different "languages," meanings, and expressions of love.

Unfortunately, "love" is idealized and glorified as a singular entity in most societies. By comparison to these idealizations of "love," reality usually falls short. People seem to yearn for a love that is pure and has no conditions. This yearning often reflects the idealized image of love expressed between mother and child. The mother is seen as having no needs or requirements, so only as the giver of love. Selfish wants and needs are considered to be contaminants of pure "love."

"Unconditional love" is therefore viewed as "true love." The belief is that if love has conditions then it must be contaminated by selfishness, so it has no value.

A significant premise here is that *conditions are not negative*. Buying and selling occurs on all levels and in all exchanges experienced in life. To be selfish and concerned with one's own welfare is natural and appropriate. Any extreme levels of emotion create disharmony and change the balance of communications. All exchanges between humans can include conditions with appropriate levels and for all occasions.

The give and take of "love," in particular, is fraught with conditions, some of which are conscious while some are unconscious. Profound and honest caring demands that the conditions of love and of being loved are expressed openly and without reservations. Negotiations and modifications can always be employed to tailor and enhance agreements. Hidden agendas in the exchanges of caring are toxic factors. Any subterfuge that confounds the desired conditions and intentions contains alienating components. Therefore, everyone has conditions. The courage to be open and forthright about the desired conditions is what love is all about. Hopefully, extending that openness to negotiations in order to expand the parameters so that they include the differences between people will help to build long-lasting bonds.

When "love" is expressed as an obsession, it is no longer about caring for another.

Obsessive "love" is an expression of deep insecurity and self-absorption. The recipient is no longer seen as a person but rather an object to be owned and possessed at all costs. The humanity and desires of the recipient have no significance for the obsessed "lover." Acquiescence and surrender are demanded. Jealousies and insecurities run rampant within the emotions of the obsessed "lover." The recipient may confuse the domination and possessive attentiveness of the "lover" as proof of intense romantic love. Teenage girls and women in patriarchal cultures often view possession as love. However, these kinds of connections often lead to dysfunction, abuse, hate, and abandonment.

Hate is experienced when the love-object refuses to be possessed by the "lover." If the recipient surrenders and is possessed, then the humanity of that individual will be gradually extinguished. The natural movement toward health and wellbeing is to find liberation and to separate from these types of dysfunctional connections.

ଔଔଔ

Personal Myths

As discussed previously, most beliefs are formed in childhood. When an adult is in conflict with a life experience, it is mostly due to their original mindsets which dictate behavior and attitudes that no longer apply to a person's current life. But, because these beliefs have a long-standing history and are habituated within the personality, it is difficult for an individual to comprehend their ineffectiveness. Internal scripts from childhood configure beliefs into dictums and command specific behavior. These internal scripts are revered as "truths" and become the personal myths within a person's psychology.

For example: the internal script or personal myth of a codependent personality can dictate the belief that it is impossible to be truly loved and wanted by another person. The codependent will then embark on a mission to create relationships and connections whereby they become needed and are assumed to be indispensable.

Another example is that of a ruthless person who operates with the belief that the only way to succeed is to cheat and beat their opponent because they can never be smart enough to compete on an equal terrain.

Or a person can believe that they are incapable of taking good care of themselves; therefore, they need to outsmart and manipulate others for the job.

Personal myths rule and conduct the inner lives of people. They comprise a private resolve and lie deeply buried within the person. These mindsets orchestrate and conduct the individual's internal scripts, so that person is compelled to choose life experiences and relationships that play out their personal myths and relive the dictums. This behavior perpetuates and validates the truth of their myths over and over. It is only through intervention and self-discovery that the scripts can stop, and the personal myths can be revised and rewritten. Identifying personal myths and understanding their implications in behavior is usually a powerful and transformative experience.

ଔଔଔଔ

Change and Timing

Current and past theories in psychology define and discuss the concept of change from a variety of perspectives. At the heart of these discussions are philosophical questions about "free will." Whether someone recognizes "free will" or not will determine how change takes place. Changes in personality, however, are difficult to comprehend and measure. Fear of feeling pain is the major deterrent to considering change. Most people hold on to what they know even if it is dysfunctional. The safety of what is known is mostly preferred to the exploration of the unknown.

A primary premise in this book is that changes, if they occur, are *expressed in attitudes*. Attitude changes are definitely possible, and are sought throughout the therapeutic process.

A change in attitude can be observed when behavior and actions verify a difference. Usually a shift occurs first in a client's self-concept. They react to the shift by changing preexisting attitudes; this then translates into a difference in behavior.

Significant life experiences can also contribute to changes in attitudes as can crucial events and discoveries.

Any situation can be viewed from different angles. For example: a person's reaction to a chronic illness or the loss of a body part may cause depression. If they change their attitude, however, they may also redefine the depression that has resulted from their initial reaction to the illness. The attitude change can lead the depressed person to connecting with positive life forces that help to dissipate their depression and inspire an energized new attitude. The aim of psychotherapy is to help create fresh, energized attitudes toward the self and to change responses that are debilitating.

The psychotherapist cannot impose changes in a client's attitudes. Only the individual's personal internal "timing" can determine why, where, and how a shift in an attitude will occur.

As discussed above, everyone has their own sense of "timing" for the implementation of new resolutions and for their "readiness" for changes in behavior. The psychotherapist merely plays the role of tracker and pathfinder. Sensitivity toward a patient's "timing" and "readiness" is essential for effective outcomes.

The brain is much faster and more intelligent about grasping problems in a given situation than emotions. Emotions operate on more primitive levels. Unfortunately, however, in the final analysis, the *emotions rule and direct behaviors*. "Timing" and "readiness" cannot be evaluated based on the verbiage and articulations expressed by the brain; they must be seen in the behaviors that reflect an individual's actions. For example: a wife who is very angry with her cheating husband and threatens to leave the marriage nevertheless remains in the same situation; she is indicating that she is not "ready" to leave, no matter how difficult the circumstances. She will leave only when she is "ready" to take that step. Once she has left the situation, we can then observe a realized "change" in her attitude. In this respect, "change" and "timing" are closely connected. Change is only possible when a person's internal timing is in accordance with making it.

Understanding and respecting a patient's timing for change is of the utmost importance. If a patient is pushed toward a change before their "readiness" is present, the therapist's efforts will eventually backfire and lose their effectiveness.

ରୋରୋରୋ

Three Major Driving Centers

The impetus for behaviors, motivations, and movements seems to be centered, metaphorically, in three areas of the body: the mind, the heart, and the genitals. These three centers exist, operate, and interact within any given individual. However, most people are inclined toward emphasizing one center primarily, or the interactions between just two of the three. A harmonious balance among all three centers is the most desirable state to achieve.

The "mind" represents the intellect; the "heart" is the symbol for feelings; and the "genitals" represent drives and actions. For example: people who are inclined toward the "mind" are more intellectual; those whose heart is more in focus are emotional and affectionate; and people who are driven by their genitals are more action-oriented.

The combinations of these centers make for interesting observations and conjectures. The person who has a strong connection between his/her mind and his/her heart but is weaker in connecting with his/her genitals may exhibit tendencies toward being smart, articulate, and caring. He/she would not be a person of action; instead he/she would come across as more of a dreamer or someone who has a lot of ideas that he/she does not implement.

The person who is more connected to his/her mind and genitals than his/her heart usually demonstrates good intellect and action but appears less caring and compassionate. The person who is more connected to his/her heart and genitals and less to his/her mind may present as someone who falls in love frequently, but recklessly, and without much forethought.

There are other possible permutations of these centers and how a person's tendencies translate into behavior. However, these conjectures are more interesting and less factual; they describe various character emphases in people's behaviors. What is more useful is finding ways to create a healthy balance between mind, heart, and genitals, and to strengthen any weaker centers as a way of bringing them into sync.

ଚ୍ଚଚ୍ଚ

Mind-Body Connections

The connections between the mind and body become very apparent in the practice of psychotherapy. When a person is physically ill or handicapped, their moods, attitudes, and psychological wellbeing are also altered. When a person experiences mental conflicts, their immune system and physical health are also compromised. Physical wellbeing changes mental attitudes; mental wellbeing promotes healthy directions in the body. Both medical and psychological treatments have consequent effects on the mind and the body.

Essential Premises

Unfortunately, most physicians evaluate illness from a purely physical and biological perspective; while psychologists tend to assume that the mind is at the root of most dysfunctions within the body.

The premise of these essays is that the mind and body are interactive and connected. Behaviors and attitudes can change physical health. Concomitantly, reactions to physical conditions can revise a person's mental views and behaviors.

Therefore, it is essential to consider a person as a whole, seeing all of their physical and mental aspects as interactive. Biology and the environment plus a person's genetic blueprint, education, aspirations, and attitudes, all pool together to constitute and impact someone's behavior.

ෙෙෙ

Gender Disputes

Men and women have different orientations toward fulfilling their desires, just as they have different physical bodies and ways of expressing their needs. However, everyone seems to *want* the same things: love, recognition, health, success, and wellbeing. These are core hopes to which everyone aspires. *How to achieve these aspirations* is where differences between genders are most apparent.

For example: women strive to achieve closeness through verbal encounters; they use touch to express their affection. Men, on the other hand, connect better while involved in an activity. Both men and women desire actions that create closeness, but the ways in which these connections are made and maintained differ between the sexes.

There is a more detailed discussion of gender difference in the essay *The Male/Female Spectrum*.

ଜ୍ୟୋ୍ୟୋ

The Fresh Encounter

It is important to encounter the patient at each session as if it is a fresh, new meeting. There are several significant reasons for this.

Seeing each session with fresh eyes will create for the therapist the opportunity to detect minute changes, to better observe nuances, and to gather information from different perspectives. By contrast, reviewing notes before a session and seeing the patient based on previous evaluations can prejudice the psychotherapist, and fail to permit the patient to present himself/herself in a new light. Being disciplined about this "fresh look" helps the therapist clear his/her mind, be fully available, and prevent the interference of his/her own counter-transference.

Implicit in this approach to encounters between therapist and patient are the teaching and modeling suggestions that ensure fluidity and the highest probability for change. Nothing is written in stone. The possibility to reinvent the self and choose new directions is present at all times.

Another teaching implication for the therapist who takes this approach is that of modeling his/her being to be fully present in the moment. While the past exists and the future is in the forecast, it is the present that holds meaning and commands the therapist's complete attention.

ଔଔଔଔ

Veis Djalali

CONSTRUCTIVE COMMUNICATION

Communication is the exchange of a message between a communicator and a receiver. The communicator is responsible for the content and how and in what manner the messages are relayed. Provided that the receiver's attention has been captured, the receiver has the option to listen, respond, react, and/or be influenced.

People are interested mostly in expressing themselves rather than in taking the position of the listener. Even when attempting to listen, the mind has a tendency to wander and be distracted by other thoughts. Listeners usually focus on the aspects of messages that pertain to them; they also look for opportunities to revert attention back to what is self-serving.

Psychotherapists are in demand primarily because the profession involves listening, tending, and paying close attention to what is or is not being expressed. To listen requires patience, interest, and caring. Unfortunately, true listening is not the objective of communication in our modern lifestyles. Most communications are conducted on superficial levels. It is the ego primarily that conducts these exchanges. The ego's involvement in the process of communication is characterized by its motives to gain power and attention, to compete and win a designated prize, and/or to claim a larger portion of time.

Miscommunications and misunderstandings are at the heart of most conflicts.

Constructive communication occurs when the intention, content, and manner of delivery are congruent and in sync. The appropriateness of congruency depends upon the situation and the goals of the communicator.

In human communications, intention, content, and delivery are not simple black-or-white concepts. Intention can have many layers with opposing motives. For example, a declaration of love can have the primary intention of expressing caring and warmth, yet fear of rejection, bashfulness, and the need to be the victor could be layered within the content and delivery of the message. As a result, the objective of the intention becomes clouded. Similarly, the content of a message could declare love while the intention of the message may be conquest, manipulation, or an attempt to take control of the recipient without the feelings of care and/or love. When the intention of a message is obscure and not clearly defined by its communicator, the content and delivery will become confusing and contradictory.

When the content of a message is a subterfuge, a deliberate ploy to hide its true intention, then the clues to the message's dishonesty are often apparent and revealed by the way in which the message is delivered. Using the same example, a declaration of love can be delivered in such a way as to raise doubt and suspicion in the recipient. Even if the words convey love, the delivery may be cold, unfeeling, or just a little off. The receiver might also project insecurities and personal issues of their own, which result in their not being able to hear any message accurately.

Most people register the way that a message is delivered more deeply than they do the content, even when the content suggests something different. Intentions are usually more difficult to decipher. Intentions are situational and culturally regulated, especially in adults. By contrast, intentions are clearly visible in children. Young people have not yet had enough life experience to learn to be defended and adept at hiding true intentions. Adults learn quickly not to show their hands until adequate safety measures are in place.

However, there are no guarantees in communication that protect us from being deceived, fooled, taken advantage of, or hurt. Miscommunications and misunderstandings are always possible in any human exchange.

The messages sent in communications are also affected by a speaker's body language, vocal tone, emphasis, inflection, and unconscious gestures. These are all reflected in a communicator's delivery and can be clues to the speaker's intentions. The consummate actor can alter their unconscious communications, then redirect and orchestrate the delivery of their message to hide a true intention. Most sociopaths and psychopaths are adept at manipulating and controlling the delivery of their communications for the purposes of deception, as well.

In business, the intention of many communications is to seduce the consumer into buying products and spending money. The content and delivery of many business communications are designed to hide true intentions so as to increase the sale of products.

The goal in politics is to win favors and appeal to what is expected. The content and delivery of political communications are designed to persuade and convince in order to obtain support and to win elections.

In intimacy and friendship, the congruency of communication becomes more significant. Trust and caring can only be built, counted upon, and cherished through congruency.

Meta-communication is the communication *about* a communication. Meta-communication exists in the nonverbal realms. It is how a communication is received and the assumptions that it precipitates. It can confirm or contradict the intentions, contents, and delivery of a message. The perceptiveness of the receiver plays a large role in the correct and accurate receipt of any messages.

Incongruence of communication between individuals who are involved with one another and, hence, are hurt or confused by miscommunications and misunderstanding, becomes an issue in psychotherapy. Conflicts also develop when people do not take the time to listen fully. Assumptions are often made that are incorrect. Behaviors and actions that arise from false assumptions can weave a web of misleading realities that cause much grief and misunderstanding. Other common consequences of not listening and attending well include jumping to conclusions and rushing to judgment.

Examples of incongruent communications are too numerous to cite. Some are caused deliberately; others are delivered unconsciously. For instance, an individual might want to communicate caring and support yet their tone of delivery is didactic and critical. In this instance, the intention to care and be supportive misfires, even though the meta-communication transmits warmth. In another example, a spouse may express everlasting love but secretly be conducting serial infidelities. The meta-communication should warn the recipient that something is off.

Individuals can also be incongruent within their own psychology and behaviors. There might be so many various desires and goals within one individual that their intentions are multifaceted and confusing. If the intentions of self are not clear to the individual, then the content and delivery of their communications will also appear confused. For the wellbeing of one's mental health, it is very important to know one's priorities and to acknowledge the true intentions of the self. The content and delivery of intentions are secondary and are political choices to be made in terms of the context and situations that will define the appropriateness of any communication. As long as an individual is in touch with who they are and what they want, what else occurs is merely the method devised to implement those intentions.

Authenticity and congruency are significant for psychotherapy. Not only are they the means for modeling constructive communication by the psychotherapist, but they also build trust and reliability within the patient/therapist relationship. Most severely disturbed patients cannot tolerate any kind of lie or untruth in communications. Even when the communication of a disturbed patient is in code or is fragmented and difficult to comprehend, they are still able to grasp the authentic, congruent, and truthful messages that are expressed by another person, and they will respond more positively. Therefore, if constructive communication is to occur between people, the art is to be congruent with intention, content, and delivery, and also to be able to listen well. Meta-communications will project the authenticity of the communicator.

രുരുരു

Case Study: Dorothea

The following case study is a description of **Dorothea**, whose communication style was dysfunctional at all three levels of intention, content, and delivery.

Dorothea emanated warmth, liveliness, and caring; however, it was very difficult to understand her conversation when she attempted to relay a concern. Her communication style was defensive. She explained and excused, contradicted and backtracked. The subject matter was often lost in the translation of her words. The meta-communication clearly sent was, "Like me, believe me, don't judge me, and be on my side." It was as if her expectation was to be disbelieved and judged harshly. She projected guilt; she acted as though she had been captured and her attempts were to feverishly try to talk her way out of bondage in order to gain freedom.

This internal script seemed to be at the heart of all of her communications, even when the mundane was being conveyed. Dorothea's internal anxieties ruled her behavior and could be easily triggered. Most of the realities that she experienced were interpreted through these defensive lenses. It was difficult to breach the sturdy self-protective walls that she had built long ago. The dichotomies presented in her persona were very confusing. In one respect, Dorothea was charming, inviting, and attracted positive attention. In another, she baffled, frustrated, and distracted anyone who wanted to know, and get close, to her.

After months of psychotherapy, Dorothea's story began to emerge in confusing fragments. When she was five, her uncle on her mother's side sexually molested her and coerced her into secrecy. After a number of painful episodes, she confided in her mother, but her mother punished her severely and called her a wicked, lying child. At that early age, whatever foundation Dorothea had built for her self-concept shattered. Her mother, who was the most trusted and beloved person in her life, had not believed her and had called her a liar.

Dorothea's demeanor after the age of five became furtive. She went into hiding and embarked on building fortifications and defense systems. She also began to doubt and disbelieve her own reactions, thoughts, and assumptions. Her outward mission seemed to be to convince others to believe her. Every time she accomplished this goal, she gained a brief reprieve and a false sense of validation.

The relationship dynamic that came forth in psychotherapy was a cat-and-mouse game. If the therapist attempted to clarify a communication and pinpoint a parameter, Dorothea evaded and ran, daring the therapist to catch her. If the therapist stood still and did not give chase, Dorothea became her most charming and tried to seduce the therapist for attention. The only acceptable method for giving Dorothea attention was to engage and participate in a chase.

Surprisingly, Dorothea was able to hear and absorb the therapeutic work, but it had to be on her terms. She would not, or could not, react in the moment. She would take home any materials offered to her and then process them privately and singularly. It was evident in the sessions that followed that she had considered and digested what had taken place during the previous sessions.

Understanding Dorothea's need to hide her feelings in the immediate moment and to process privately was a significant discovery. In order to win further trust and effectively continue the work, the therapist had to accept and incorporate Dorothea's inability to be upfront in the moment. The work had to be telegraphed in this manner; Dorothea would then respond at a later date, in accordance with her timing.

Dorothea's intentions were to connect, to build genuine friendships, and to attract appropriate attention. However, she was riddled with fears and self-doubt that clouded and confused her projections of these intentions. The content of her communication was jumbled and contradictory. She had a style of canceling whatever she presented and never landed on any solid ground. Her delivery was charming, warm, and attractive. The meta-communication was "Like me but don't touch me or get too close." These styles of communication were in accord and consistent with the psychology she presented.

ൟൟൟ

Psychological Dynamics

In order for Dorothea to learn about being congruent, her sense of self had to be rebuilt and strengthened. Her mother inadvertently labeled Dorothea as a liar at the age of five. Ever since that point, the boundary between truth and lies had become blurry and indistinct for Dorothea. She experienced severe anxiety whenever she confronted a situation that required a truth or a lie. She learned to express both and neither simultaneously in order to feel safe. After the molestation by her trusted uncle followed by her mother's subsequent disbelief and lack of support, Dorothea's primary coping mechanisms became finding methods to feel safe.

Truths and lies were vague notions for her, yet they were also red flags in her mind; she endured the ramifications of both reactions. She had been punished when she told the truth about her molestation, *and* she had suffered when the molestation was kept a secret and turned into a lie.

As a grown woman, Dorothea was sometimes unsure whether or not the molestation had actually happened. In some instances, she re-experienced the horrors; the images were once again vivid. At other times, the memories were dim and felt like a movie that she had once seen. Her uncle, the molester, had a revered presence in her family and household. He and his family, her cousins, were all involved in her life and socialized at events as though the injury had never been committed. She often wondered if she had made up the entire story.

Dorothea grew up acquiring many other labels besides that of "liar." She was a party girl and not taken too seriously. She was a flake, and someone not to be counted on. She was a shopaholic; she had a voracious appetite for pretty clothes. She was also labeled as bright, lively, artistic, and a free spirit. As a thirty-five-year-old adult, she had had two failed marriages and had drifted from one job to another.

To help Dorothea develop a positive self-concept out of the ashes of injury and the betrayal by those closest to her, she needed to connect to the five-year-old child who remained locked up within her psyche. Dorothea had to learn to become the guardian, mother, father, teacher, and protector of that child. While growing up, she consistently blamed, ostracized, and shunned that child, just as others had done. Dorothea had to draw upon and extend beyond her own resources in order to support the child and guide it toward health and wellbeing.

Reconnecting with, supporting, and validating the five-year-old child were the beginnings of the therapeutic and healing process. Other aspects of her therapy were somewhat didactic. Experiences and homework assignments had to be created wherein Dorothea could test out the differences between truths and lies. The goal was for her to develop clear and distinct definitions for both concepts. The grays in between could be explored further, once the distinctions between truth and lies were fully clarified and internalized.

Dorothea also needed to learn, from an adult's perspective, the give-and-take in situations, the cause and effects that were found in her realities, consequences, and choices. These concepts had to be reviewed and relearned.

Dorothea had lived a double life for a long time. Internally, she harbored secrets and was furtive and fearful; she had dark thoughts and emotions. Overtly, she acted out in order to appear playful and carefree. It was as if an internal program controlled her. She hid her truths and lived lies that made her unhappy. She covered up her unhappiness in order to seem giddy and fun-loving. It was a no-win situation. Yet the program was in place to defend and safeguard Dorothea from being found out, an experience synonymous for her with being devastated.

When Dorothea was a child, being safe was the primary order for survival. Those elements that constituted danger when she was little were no longer in operation in her adult life. However, she had habituated into her personality and adult behaviors those same precautions and safety measures that she had acquired for survival as a child. Reconnecting with the child within her was a method of healing the wounds that were sustained by the little girl in the molestation, along with the lies that she had been forced to live.

Realizing her strengths and attributes as an adult was a method of shrinking the power of the past and of discovering a path to the present. Current environments and situations did not demand the same safety measures that she had learned to impose upon herself in the past. The realization that Dorothea was no longer a helpless child without control or power or voice was therapeutic and healing. Discovering choice was empowering as was learning ways to be strong in her stance and to take good care of her wellbeing. As a child, Dorothea was overwhelmed and overruled. As an adult, she could become assertive and no longer indoctrinated, if she so chose.

Dorothea's communication styles were developed to create confusion and obscurity between lies and truths. She imagined and created a place where she could express truth and lies while still remaining hidden. In this respect, she believed that she had found safety. When Dorothea emerged from her past wounds in order to heal and operate in the present, she was also able to differentiate between the concepts of truth, lies, and the gray areas between them. The communication style that she had developed in the past no longer had the validity that it once had. It became viable and possible for her to develop a more positive and constructive means of communication.

ଔଔଔ

PREVALENT CONDITIONS ENCOUNTERED IN PSYCHOTHERAPY: A CONDENSED OVERVIEW

Therapists encounter a vast range of psychological conditions during the course of their training as they pursue their profession and accumulate experience. In psychotherapy, some psychological conditions are more prevalent than others and appear more frequently. This overview introduces some of these more common psychological conditions that are encountered by anyone who embarks on the journey of being or becoming a psychotherapist.

ରୁଠରୁଠ

Depression and anxiety disorders are often at the top of the list of conditions most frequently seen in psychotherapy. There is a great deal of research available for review on both of these conditions. Some consider depression and anxiety to be "brother and sister."

Sometimes, psychiatrists prescribe antidepressants and anti-anxiety drugs simultaneously when an individual suffers from aspects of both conditions. From a clinical point of view, however, the demeanor of a depressed person is very different from an anxious personality.

It is important to clarify up front that feeling sad and being melancholy are *not to be equated with clinical depression*. However, if sadness is not overcome it can eventually lead to depression. Sometimes being sad and/or nervous are appropriate responses to what is occurring in an individual's life. Therefore, the clinician has to learn to differentiate between clinical depression and anxieties that need treatment from those responses that are a natural reaction to life's happenstances.

There are many controversies in the field regarding whether dysfunctions in moods are biologically based and, hence, can or should be regulated with drugs. Those who are not advocates for medication for depression and anxiety propose talk therapies and various hands-on methods of treatment. There are also proponents of the mind/body connection. They adhere to the belief that open pathways exist between mind and body, that they are interactive, and that they carry mutually reactive components. These therapists propose that the mind and its emotions can create disease, and that physical breakdowns of the body can cause depression and other mental dysfunction.

In clinical observation, the depressed person exhibits a lack of energy; she or he is sluggish, and their zest for life is diminished to a degree that it creates concern. A therapist must assess the degree of depression in order to ward off suicidal ideations.

There are many different types of treatments for depression besides or in conjunction with medication. If there is a source for depression within an individual's psychology that is not considered inherent and/or biological, psychotherapeutic explorations can be employed to discover this source and then connect it to the behaviors presented.

ෲෲෲ

There are various types of **anxiety disorders**. An anxious person usually appears restless or agitated and finds it difficult to be focused and/or consistent. Some kind of fear or fears seems to be the controlling factor of this anxious state. Anticipating the realization of that fear causes anxiety. Avoidance mechanisms are usually devised in order to nullify the source of the fear. Unfortunately, avoidance of most fears backfires; this can aggravate the anxiety disorder. Therapeutic intervention entails the building of strength to face and defeat whatever *causes the fear* and subsequent anxiety.

Severe anxiety can lead to panic attacks and debilitating chronic phobias; these also can depress a person to varying degrees. Unlike the lack of energy that you see in a depressed person, the anxious person has an abundance of energy although it is often unfocused and expressed haphazardly, resulting in exhaustion.

There are many well-researched and effective treatment modalities for anxiety disorders. Cognitive Behavior treatments seem to be popular and practiced frequently.

ର୍ଷଷର୍ଷ

People suffering from **obsessive-compulsive behaviors** are also seen frequently in psychotherapy. It is easy to get sidetracked by the presenting problem of an obsessive individual. Usually the obsessive person is engrossed and preoccupied with the repetition of persistent behaviors and/or thoughts. These persistent thoughts and behaviors are unconsciously conceived mechanisms to defend deeper layers of suffering that are buried within the psyche. The relentless preoccupation with a task and/or thought distracts the focus away from the true center of pain that is being guarded. The obsession becomes the problem instead, and serves as a barrier or defensive fort, preventing further penetrations. If a therapist gets caught in the contents of an obsession, entrapment takes place. The therapist will then collude unwillingly in the fortification of the patient's defensive strategies.

The therapeutic goal entails unearthing the source of the patient's pain while not entertaining the content of the obsession as the problem for psychotherapy. There may be clues to observe within the obsession's content, and certain compulsive behaviors relay messages about the deeper layers of a patient's psyche. But bypassing obsessive behavior is not an easy task. Patients feel safe in their obsessive rituals. In order for a therapist to understand the defensive structures built in to obsessive-compulsive behaviors, it is helpful to first win the cooperation and trust of the patient.

ଔଔଔଔ

Loneliness and isolation are often at the heart of most unhappiness that is expressed in psychotherapy, although not usually communicated as such so directly or simply. Often these conditions are camouflaged in layers of complexities and rationalizations. Most people feel lonely when they are not connected to significant others who care and feel love for them. This lack of connection may be a reality of life, or may be self-imposed by the lonely person's inability to form connections.

The realities of life that can render a patient lonely include the loss experienced due to death, divorce, and/or other types of breakups. Evident misunderstandings and miscommunications can result in an individual being ostracized from family and community. Nonconformists also feel aspects of aloneness. Those who have been marginalized by the dominant or mainstream culture can feel isolated and disconnected, as well.

Self-imposed isolations derive from psychological components of the personality. An individual may hunger for company and/or need a significant relationship but be unable to establish one for a variety of reasons. Psychotherapy can help to determine the patient's personality characteristics that affect that person's ability to attract the deep connections that could assuage their pain of loneliness.

Oftentimes it is an individual's intensity and neediness that frighten and overwhelm others who attempt to get close. Sometimes the person has no concept of their impact on others and of how the intensity of their communication and behavior affect people around them. Talking excessively without attention to their listener's receptiveness, for example, is a common deterrent for building close relationships. A therapist can help to identify these types of characteristics that negatively impact a patient's ability to form healthy connections. The next steps in this therapeutic progress involve discovering and learning appropriate and positive behaviors that are conducive for forming connections.

ଓଓଓଓ

Abuse, with its numerous forms and implications, is a frequent topic in psychotherapy. The range of abusive behaviors is vast. It can occur in subtle, long-term violations or be demonstrated in volatile and disturbing episodes that require the intervention of law enforcement.

The definition of abuse is when a domineering force imposes control and damaging behaviors on a weaker and more recessive party without permission, invitation, and/or volition. Child abuse, domestic violence, date rapes, sexual harassments, and bullying (be it cyber or in person) are some of the common types of abuse that are seen in psychotherapy. The therapeutic task, when law enforcement is not required, is to help boost the self-concept and the self-image of the victim in order for them to develop the necessary strength to be free from the abusive relationship. Learning to stand up to an abuser is profound; acquiring strength and gumption is essential both for survival and wellbeing. Of course, when dealing with abusers who are deemed dangerous and who put their victims in jeopardy, the patient's safety should be of utmost importance.

The therapeutic task for treating the abuser is similar to treating the victim, in that this person also suffers from poor self-concepts and various inadequacies. Even if they are psychopaths and/or sociopaths, most abusers likely have had some form of victimization in their history and background. Behaviors that are controlling and that hurt others through abuse are usually *learned;* they operate as dysfunctional coping mechanisms.

The therapist who works with victims and abusers must learn to be extremely self-aware and nonjudgmental in order to be effective. Understanding the humanity and motivation of these patients is a primary focus of the therapist. Moral judgments can hinder the process of developing open, uncensored communication.

ଓଓଓଓ

Rape victims are also seen in therapy. The aim of the therapist is to help the sexually assaulted individual realize that rape is an act of violence and that the victim is in a state of trauma.

Trauma has to be treated and allowed to heal so that it does not control and affect the individual for the rest of their lives. Rape is an awful act that occurs *to* someone; it does not define or limit who that person is or can be. Helping the patient to separate the act from their being, as a person, is the first step in therapeutic healing.

Usually a rapist does not seek therapy voluntarily. Generally, when these perpetrators are encountered in psychotherapy, it is as a requirement by court or law enforcement.

A rapist may be acting out aggression or hostilities. The rapist may have poor impulse control and enjoy imposing control and causing pain. The psychological motivations of a rapist must be determined, diagnosed, and understood in order to devise therapeutic interventions.

ଈଔଈଔଈଔ

Men seem to suffer more frequently from the inability to control their anger. Women are more in touch with the variety of their feelings. By contrast, many men pool their negative feelings and reactions under one umbrella, which then translates into expressions of ***anger and aggressive behavior***.

An effective anger management program involves first helping an individual to realize that *anger is not a feeling* in itself, but, rather, is *a reaction* to a feeling or feelings. Recognizing the original feeling that has become obscured by reactive anger is a significant step for someone to take, as they learn to manage their unruly, angry impulses. For example, say that a man feels inadequate or guilty or even shy—some type of discomfort—but instead of experiencing those feelings, he can only feel impotent rage, and it frequently snowballs into an outburst. It is difficult to be constructive with a gigantic snowball that is rolling down a steep mountain! However, when the snowball can be deciphered into small, recognizable particles, the angry person can develop some understanding and then begin to take control over the miasma of emotions that causes them confusion and impotency. Acting out aggressively is propelled by reactions to feelings of helplessness generated by the inability to be constructive with the onslaught of unidentifiable emotions. The aggressive, incontrollable behaviors generally result in creating more confusion, regret, and mayhem.

There are also some women who express uncontrollable anger. The mechanisms of their behavior may be similar to a man's poor impulse control or may involve other aspects of their need to control and provoke fear in others. The psychology behind all behavior needs to be understood in the context of the complete individual in order to devise and implement an effective intervention.

ৎৎৎৎ

Often poor impulse control is associated and combined with ***drug and alcohol abuse.***

The Jekyll-and-Hyde example is often used to describe someone who is basically "good" but who becomes a "fiend" when under the influence of his or her drug of choice. Psychotherapy with drug and alcohol abusers is a difficult process. Drug and alcohol abusers are notorious liars when the disease controls them. The drug abuser is ruled foremost by the need for the drug. The cover-ups and devious behaviors that ensue can easily convince the psychotherapist to waver from the healing path and pursue lame ducks. In order for a healing path to emerge and deliver positive outcomes, the drug abuser has to be a willing participant and committed to overcoming their addiction. The full cooperation of the drug abuser is a requirement for the fight and struggle against the demons of any drug.

Every individual has their own timing for being "ready" to let go of an addiction to drugs or alcohol. It is a process that requires courage, maximum effort, and Herculean strength not to be deterred by possible slip-ups. The journey is long and arduous; it requires full commitment from both patient and therapist.

ৎৎৎৎ

Chronic illnesses and disabilities are also conditions that involve a patient's learning new skills and coping mechanisms in order for treatment to realize healthy outcomes. Common enemies of people with these afflictions are depression and the loss of the spirit to struggle through the fight. Redefining the self within the confines of a limiting disease and/or injury becomes a key factor for psychotherapy. Zest for life often measures how well a patient is able to redefine and reinvent themself in light of an injury or disability. If the zest for life is weak, the therapeutic focus needs to be on building up the patient's internal forces that can guide their will to live, to cope, and to be happy. If a zest for life already exists, then the goal for therapy is about directing these powerful energies toward viable and constructive plans for action.

The amount of time it takes for a person to react to the loss of health and/or appendages along with any disabilities that may follow, is very personal, and generally involves a process. It usually takes years for an individual to come to terms with these kinds of losses, along with their ramifications and consequences. When a person is no longer in denial about their injury and any life changes that they have sustained, then proactive behaviors and positive participation in life's processes becomes apparent. These are significant signs of their psychological recovery.

The struggle to survive within the confines of imposed limitations can have many ups and downs; major hurdles may need to be overcome. However, once the zest for life becomes dominant in a patient's psyche again, their prognosis also becomes positive.

ଓଉଓ

Midlife crises and other happenstances in life that present **opportunities for reinvention of the self** are both traumatic and healthy, in terms of expanding the self-concept to horizons not previously imagined or considered. People painstakingly develop their comfort zones over time in order to safeguard them and permit them to function comfortably within the system. These comfort zones can also stifle people and dim their lives to boring levels and to predictable proportions. When events force an individual to take note and question their choices in life, an opportunity opens up for them to accept new inputs and create new directions.

These states of being can generate anxiety, but the creative outpouring that accompanies them can also be very rewarding. Guiding a client to risk despite their feeling fear in the midst of a crisis that questions their choices and challenges the meaning of their life is the art of psychotherapy. It is appropriate to have fears and anxieties in the face of this type of existential crisis. The art of psychotherapy involves helping an individual to use these energies to construct new choices and to develop exciting new meanings and purpose for their life.

ଓଉଓ

Dysfunctions in families and ***discords in relationships*** of all kinds are often the reason for seeking therapy. In today's world, it is not unusual for people to live with multiple families with a variety of origins as a result of divorce. Attempting to live within any family dynamic can be a breeding ground for dysfunction. When multiple families are involved, the degree of dysfunction can accelerate. Issues with children and teenagers are often the major concerns of parents. The "teenager" has a unique developmental stage all of its own. When couples come together from different backgrounds and life views to form a new family, they may develop miscommunications and misunderstandings on many levels.

The relationships that form within a family and then extend into old age have many stages of development. Each one has its own trials, tribulations, and rewards. These stages of life will be discussed in more depth in subsequent chapters.

ଔଓଔଓ

There are many tangents and numerous offshoots of the conditions described above. Those that have been mentioned represent the condensed categories of issues that are most commonly seen in psychotherapy. The list of human foibles is infinite. By the time an intern in psychotherapy has concluded their required hours, he or she will have been exposed to a vast number of the human conditions, pains, encounters, follies, and mishaps. This exposure is necessary and fertile training for the preparations to become a psychotherapist.

ଔଓଔଓ

THE ORCHESTRA WITHIN

Before describing what is meant by "The Orchestra Within," the concept of the "inner child" needs to be discussed.

The notion of the "inner child" or "the child within" has been bandied about for a long time. The Freudians, Jungians, and pop psychologists like Eric Bern all reference versions of this concept and use it in their theoretical frameworks and treatment modalities.

It is extremely interesting how this concept has filtered into the public's understanding. Patients often use this expression to describe a tender and vulnerable part of themselves. It is also used to express feelings and emotions that are regarded as inappropriate in adult, mature behavior.

The concept of the inner child in clinical work is useful in identifying the wishes and impulsive desires of adults. However, when the needs and voice of the inner child are strong, there is also a voice in opposition. This voice is stern, punitive, and critical, and acts to restrain the inner child from plunging into action. This opposing voice can be called "the inner judge."

"The inner judge" embodies the critical, authoritarian aspect of the self. Its function is to pass judgment on desires, wants, and behaviors. It is mostly negative and censorial. "The inner child" is impulsive, unrestrained, and creative, but acts without forethought or consideration for any consequences. "The inner judge" and "the inner child" are in opposition and have a reactive relationship. The stronger the pull of the inner child, the harsher and more controlling the inner judge becomes. The stronger the dictums and commands of the inner judge, the more rebellious and contrary the reactions of the inner child. The inner judge knows *what is "right"* and the inner child knows *what feels good or bad*. The struggle of these two opposing powers inside a person causes conflict, anxiety, depression, and often impotency. The therapist can be effective in creating awareness of these inner characters that clearly have different functions but who need one another's input in order to act in a balanced way.

The inner child brings desire and inspiration into the system of the personality, but needs the guidance of the judge in order to see danger, obstacles, and consequences before leaping into action.

The dynamic between the inner judge and the inner child describes an interactive structure within the self, rather than any singular force. Therefore, in clinical work, the concept of "the inner child" by itself is too simplistic. Many feelings and emotions are pooled beneath the umbrella of the "inner child" concept; it is much more effective, however, if a person's feelings and needs are identified separately, with emotions acknowledged independently along with their roles, meanings, and impact within the composite of a given personality.

For example, the needs of "child" and "judge" are in opposition, hence, pulling the individual in different directions. This usually creates discomfort, disharmony, and confusion. By identifying the needs separately and then by understanding their roles and purpose, the value and necessity of each need becomes apparent, and their positive and negative ramifications can be clarified.

The therapist can guide, demonstrate, and problem-solve various examples that demonstrate how collaboration and unity can exist between these opposing needs. When any one need is ignored, then the balance and natural flow can become off-kilter.

The first step in this therapeutic problem-solving process is to see the inner child and the inner judge distinctly, and to understand their function and operation within the psychic system. The second step is to observe how they collide, oppose, and generate chaos in the system. The therapist can be helpful here by opening the pathways for collaborative and unified interaction between the judge and child, as an alternative to the dysfunctional state that ensues when they are in opposition.

When a patient has grasped an understanding of the dynamics between these two major opposing forces within the self, they have in place the groundwork for seeing the larger picture. The therapist can then begin to introduce the notion that there are many more forces within the self besides just the child and the judge. All of these needs can be discovered and identified, with their voices and purposes heard equally, and then woven into the fabric of the self. As this specific and detailed picture develops, cohesion can take place.

This image is never stagnant: it is sketched and re-sketched in an evolving self. It is out of this dynamic that the notion of the "orchestra within" takes shape.

ଓ୨ଓ୨ଓ୨

The image of the "orchestra within" is one that conveys a body of players who have different sounds, needs, and purposes. They come together with their differences to harmonize and create beautiful music. Each player has his or her own particular function and importance within the whole body of the orchestra. The inner judge and child are part of the orchestra. They are important voices; but they do not control the orchestra.

A conductor is needed on the podium: an overseer, or the objective part of a person that sees the larger picture of the full orchestra at all times. The conductor's function is to know and hear all the sounds (needs) in order to create harmony and beautiful music.

Most people are unaware of their objective overseer. They tend to be enmeshed in a particular need or conflict that they feel in the moment. Their problem-solving abilities are reduced to black or white. At this point, they seem to be clueless that the needs and functions that seem to divide them can, in fact, come together and collaborate at a roundtable-type discussion. Negotiations and then a solution *can* be realized and achieved without having a "winner" or a "loser."

The overseer—the conductor, the mother host—can always see the larger picture which includes all of the individual's various needs along with their play, in behavior. The overseer gives equal attention and care to all of its parts. It can build bridges and create connections between different needs. The patient can be guided to know that being torn between their needs is a *dysfunctional position*. Options and choices are available if the larger picture can be accessed; if not, they risk being ruled by one or two needs that obscure the sight and vision of the full orchestra within.

The overseer's job is to help all of the factions equally, in the spirit of cooperation and harmony, in order to arrive at an appropriate, doable choice that is best for the whole organism, not just one part or particular need. For example: I want to have fun and play rather than work. Two separate needs: work versus play. The task is to come up with a program that allows ample time for work and yet creates time for fun and joy. This mode advocates that the need to be responsible and work is important but that the need to have fun is also important. In the spirit of cooperation, the individual can create a program that includes sufficient time for work and play; this will benefit me as a whole person.

At the appropriate time, when the patient is ready, this concept of the orchestra within can be introduced. A therapist can set the stage by helping his or her patient visualize their own individualized concept of an internal orchestra, one that includes all the various instruments, players, and sounds that are unique to that person's psyche.

The "orchestra" is a metaphor for the many voices, needs, and emotions that reside within an individual's personality. Most people are quick to see in the orchestra the critical and impulsive parts of themselves. As noted previously, it is easiest for the therapist to start the process with what is most accessible for their patient, so they can begin with the images of the child and judge. After that, it may take a number of sessions before a client can fully identify their other characters. It's not necessary to identify all the voices and characters completely. This is a work in progress, impacted by a person's effort and development. There are some characters that are present throughout life, others that come and go, and some that remain yet to be discovered.

When a patient has identified as many characters as seem pertinent for the moment, their next step is to get to know these characters as fully as possible: to actually hear their voices and identify their wants. A useful diagnostic tool is to have a patient visualize and give form to these aspects of themselves. If their conceptualizations are fuzzy, then perhaps more work is needed in order to develop better self-awareness.

For example: many see a clown, a doubting Thomas, green-eyed envy, a raging monster, a fearful pipsqueak, and a good Samaritan as characters within their "orchestra." Where appropriate, it may help a patient to encourage them to see these aspects of themselves in terms of historical characters, film personalities, and even colors, animals, edibles, or objects. The stronger the images generated, the better the patient's ability to know their characters and, hence, the more progress will be achieved in therapy.

When a person's characters begin to take form in their awareness, they will then be able to hear their voices and sounds. Usually these inner characters clamor for attention and expression. Some voices are exceptionally strong, in fact, and can drown or dominate the weaker needs. At this point, the patient often experiences a dizzying confusion, disorder, fragmentation of self, and loss of control; this can lead to a standstill and impotence. For the therapist, this is a significant juncture—an opportunity to introduce the *need for a conductor* for this orchestra within. The conductor can be constructed as an entity capable of taking charge and harmonizing the factions in order to create beautiful music.

Most people are perplexed by the notion of a conductor. They have never imagined an aspect of themselves that can see the larger picture and run the entire show. When they come to understand the need for such a figure, many people rush to put their judge in the position of conductor; they see the judge as the best candidate to serve as leader of their orchestra. Indeed, the judge is strong and forceful, comfortable in rendering judgments, and content to be in power. Unfortunately, that is the *worst possible choice.*

The judge is a two-dimensional aspect of self and does not have the ability to view the larger picture. A good deal of the work in therapy then becomes to de-throne this judge and shrink him/her back into a size to fit in one seat in the orchestra. The judge merely represents another voice, not the leader of them. This process can be a struggle, however, and no easy task. Habitually, most "good" men and women are accustomed to being guided by a stern inner judge. And "bad" men and women are used to having their inner child run the show.

The "conductor" or the "benevolent overseer" emerges when a patient comes to view the self as a larger picture. When the complexity of this entity is fully realized, the notion of a guardian, caretaker or overseer begins to make good sense. The overseer's role is to exist for the wellbeing of *all* of the different facets. Its job is to be impartial, non-judgmental, and objective. Its work is to benefit all the parts through collaboration and harmony.

It is very important for the therapist to demonstrate this role of conductor within the personality dynamic by providing the patient with problem-solving examples. She or he can illustrate how, with the emergence of a conductor, a person's other voices recede back into their orchestra seats to play their own significant roles in order to be heard, but do not take control of the orchestra. The voices in the orchestra are not objective; they are two-dimensional and can only express their particular need without regard for the larger picture. These characters are incapable of ruling with objectivity and impartiality.

In the construction of the conductor or overseer, a pathway can take hold that leads to a sense of wholeness, cohesion, and effective internal dynamic. The conductor is able to harmonize with care, appropriateness, resolution and wisdom, and give equal attention to the various demands in a psyche. When this happens, the voices inside feel recognized, heard and valued, resulting in a blending of needs into a cohesive complexity; this in turn translates into constructive action.

A patient can be guided to see himself or herself as a host that contains a variety of needs and emotions. All of these needs are valid; each one plays an important role in the development and welfare of the whole being. Some of these voices are not "nice," but they do have value. It is important to demonstrate the pros and cons of each facet, along with how they relate to and need one another in order to survive successfully within the composite self. For instance, anger is a dark emotion but can be appropriate and useful in certain circumstances, or it can be inappropriate and debilitating in other situations.

This metaphor—"the orchestra within"—can describe and explain our multifaceted structure in a picturesque manner. Struggles, from something small to big events, can be divided into needs and voices in order to better understand them. Feeling stuck or unable to make a choice, or choosing a direction that results in too much loss, can be perceived as a situation where needs and opposing emotions are in a state of chaos, lacking a "conductor" to lead them and create cooperation. The visual image of the "orchestra within" with a benevolent conductor at the podium, who is able to harmonize the struggles of the needs, can be an inspiring and rewarding sense of wholeness and wellbeing.

ର୍ଥ୍ୟର୍ଥ

Case Study: Madeline

The following case study exemplifies how this method works.

Madeline was born in Geneva, Switzerland. She was young, beautiful, wealthy, cultured, well-traveled, and educated. She had been in a relationship with a man in his late forties since the age of twenty. She was twenty-three years old at the time of this case; he had two daughters around her same age. They all lived together in a house that he owned. However, Madeline paid rent for her portion of the living expenses and had purchased a good deal of the furniture. She was vague and defensive when she described his character. It appeared that he was involved in shady business practices and growing marijuana in his backyard with no regard for the risk to which he subjected Madeline and his daughters.

She captured this man's attention when he was involved with a friend of hers. She became deeply enamored and fell in love, seeing him more as a guru or mentor, and placing him high up on a pedestal in her mind. She remained guilt-ridden about her friend, yet also felt victorious about successfully nabbing him for herself.

Madeline left her parents' home in Geneva and traveled across the world to live with this man. During their years of cohabitation, while under his influence, she came to feel angry with her parents and alienated from them. Her communications with her parents became volatile, which created more distance and unhappiness. Needless to say, her parents highly disapproved of their daughter's relationship with this "old man."

During the course of psychotherapy, Madeline expressed feelings of rage, anxiety, and depression. She wasn't sure how she felt about the boyfriend. She experienced rage primarily during sex with him, and felt mostly tongue-tied, petulant, and unable to understand or express her own feelings and reactions. She appeared to be in a total state of confusion: in pain and unconscious of her internal dynamics. She also carried severe tension pain in her shoulders. She declared, "I think I need to leave this relationship. Edward isn't who I thought he was. But the idea of leaving devastates me. I don't know how I can do it!"

Upon further investigation, it was discovered that Madeline had abandonment issues from childhood. She was the only girl child, the youngest sibling of three brothers. Her parents traveled and partied a good deal, so she was often left in the care of nannies and boarding schools. The notion of any kind of separation, ending, or major change triggered mountains of anxiety. In order to be with Edward, she had left her home, defied her parents, and changed her lifestyle—everything that was most difficult for her to do. So she felt very attached and committed; but her feelings for him as her man were wavering.

Being so invested in her relationship with Edward, she often balked or clammed-up when questions arose about Edward's character or when scrutiny was applied toward his shady practices or risky behavior. The therapeutic strategy that best suited her at that point was to leave her situation with Edward alone and instead to focus primarily on building her inner strength and self-confidence. By promoting her self-esteem, she would become capable of making good choices for herself. Therefore, "the orchestra within" seemed to be the most appropriate therapeutic exercise.

Madeline's internal struggles revealed the following characters who were playing their various instruments as embodied in her "orchestra within": the princess; the huntress; the lost, innocent little girl; the slut or sex goddess; the artist; the altruistic visionary; the successful businesswoman; and, of course, the harsh critic in the position of power, ruling the entire orchestra mercilessly. The players were all interesting characters with strong opposing views, each pushing to be attended to and, hence, generating disorder and chaos.

The voice and needs of these characters pronounced the following:

The *princess* needed to be adored, worshiped, cherished, and taken care of in accordance with her affluent upbringing. Edward felt short in this department. He was a good talker; but in action, she was taking care of him, at least financially.

This part of her was sorely neglected, and comingled with the old myth from childhood—that maybe she wasn't worthy of being taken care of.

The *huntress* was a bold part of her who was single-minded and had both the power and impetus to win. This was demonstrated by Madeline's ability to compete for Edward's attention with an equally young, pretty woman, and by being victorious.

However, this part of her had receded into the background as she became dominated by Edward's beliefs as well as by her need to please him. She was also awed and a little afraid of this part of her, someone who could be so "bad." Her altruistic side believed in being "good": playing fair and with honor. This dichotomy between the huntress and the humanitarian caused guilt and grief in her system.

Her *visionary altruistic side* believed in creating a better universe that conserved energy, recycled refuse, and connected with all people as brothers and sisters. Though this side of hers was highly valued, it lacked power and drive to take action. It was gentle and "nice" without being assertive. Madeline didn't realize that the visionary needed to collaborate with the huntress's abilities in order for ventures to be successful.

The *lost, innocent little girl* felt totally incapable of having movement, action, and potency in the world. She wanted "good" parental connections that would take care of her and make wise decisions for her. She had erroneously believed that Edward would play that role in her life. She equated parental care with love from a mate. Mostly she felt pain, disappointment, low self-esteem, loss, and hurt. She didn't see herself as victim but rather as an unequipped baby in the woods.

The *sex goddess or slut* had strong sexual desires and looked for a partner who could fully satisfy her. She had a hard time expressing her desires. She acted aloof but secretly was capable of doing anything. In her imagination she was a femme fatale, but in action, she described herself as quite conservative. The sex goddess also needed the power of the huntress to come out and be expressed.

The *artist* had many wonderful creative talents. She painted, did crafts and photography, created gardens, and felt happy in these endeavors. Unfortunately, she didn't know how to translate her creative energies into a viable profession or business enterprise. It wasn't enough for her just to be an artist. She needed to prove to herself, to her parents, and to Edward that she could stand on her own in the world.

The *successful businesswoman* was ambitious. She struggled with numerous ideas and ventures, hoping to hit the jackpot. She wanted to prove that, even though she had a trust fund and did not need to work, she could be worthy and successful and independent.

The *harsh critic* mostly pronounced fears and obstacles about every inspiration or thought that Madeline contemplated. The judge rendered her immobile and impotent by overwhelming her with the voice of doom and failure. If she thought about leaving her situation with Edward, the critic scared her into believing that she would not be able to handle life without him. Heavy criticisms knocked down any business venture that was put on the table. The judge managed to bring Madeline to a standstill at every turn.

ଓଔଔଔ

Psychological Dynamics

As these characters within Madeline's internal orchestra became more vocal and concrete through therapy, she began to see how they worked in opposition to one another, rather than in collaboration. Seeing these characters in full form and with their individual sounds and needs helped Madeline to own these aspects of her psyche as meaningful parts in the larger picture of her entire orchestra. It became obvious how these parts needed one another in order to devise and implement constructive behaviors.

The needs were interdependent and strong when they acted together as a unit to express movement and good survival behaviors. The judge or the harsh critic could not be put in the position of power and leadership because that place belonged to an overseer/guardian/conductor who was capable of composing harmony without judgment or harshness through care, benevolence, and objectivity. The critic had to be replaced and then put into the orchestra; a conductor had to be created to organize the good of all her parts and bring unity to the picture. When the conductor emerged and was placed in a position of control, orchestrating the internal needs of the full orchestra, she would discover a sense of calm and order.

Here, the therapist could model how the various aspects of self can collaborate in behavior. For example, "the huntress" carried power but needed "the visionary," "the artist," and the "businesswoman" to supply direction and motive. The "visionary," "the artist" and the "businesswoman" could generate ideas but would be impotent to act without the power of the "huntress." "The businesswoman" could guide and modify the inspirations of "the artist" and "the visionary" toward concrete and viable ventures.

As the collaborative efforts of the huntress, businesswoman, and the visionary translated into successful behavior, the needs of "the princess" and "the lost, innocent, little girl" would be parented internally, resulting in fulfillment and self-esteem. The "harsh judge" would have less intensity and power when positioned in an orchestra seat rather than in the role of conductor. The conductor could call on the "judge" to give advice and be useful when needed. "The sex goddess" required the confidence of the other voices to enable her to articulate her particular voice and needs. If she remained in silence with her desired self-expressions censored, she would feel dissatisfied.

ଔଔଔଔ

When a patient demonstrates an understanding of their own picture of the orchestra, its players and how they connect, interact, collaborate, and negotiate, with an overseer at the helm 24/7, the therapist can feel assured that this metaphor has been an effective means to strengthening the inner resources of their patient toward health and wellbeing.

෧෬෬෧

Veis Djalali

BUILDING A BRIDGE

In the establishment of a relationship, certain inevitable developmental stages occur. This seems to be true universally and regardless of the type of relationship, be it heterosexual or homosexual, friendship, business, or filial. Only siblings have a unique dynamic particular to them. These stages of development reflect the progress as to how people come together into relationship. This essay focuses primarily on the *second stage of development* in any type of dyad connection. The second stage describes the building blocks of the relationship. Psychotherapeutic intervention has the potential to be most successful at the beginning of this period, when it can implant worthy tools that can be used throughout the couple's life.

Briefly, the first stage of any relationship is the biological/psychological attraction that sparks interest and marks the beginning. This has been written about extensively, and no definitive explanation has been ascertained as to why people find one another attractive and/or are drawn to one other. A liaison may also begin for other reasons without this feeling of initial attraction. The participants in question may have complicit agreements for rational and pragmatic reasons, or one of any number of other purposes for coming together without feeling the ineffable chemistry. Whether a relationship is formed as the result of an attraction or has a concrete, pragmatic purpose, the stages that follow are similar in sentiment and psychology for all.

In the first stage of a relationship, there are usually projections of hope, excitement, and positive expectations. Couples tend to give one another the benefit of the doubt, make excuses for conflicts between them, and be blind to bad behavior. Literature refers to this first stage as the *"honeymoon period"*; it can last from a month to a year. This is a period for tasting and considering the possibilities. While getting acquainted occurs initially, tests of the durability and sustainability of the bonds formed characterize the second developmental stage.

This second stage is the *actual formation of the relationship* from a more realistic, down to earth perspective. The honeymoon glow has diminished and, by this time, the couple has taken each other's measure. They don't see one another through rose-colored glasses anymore. They undertake the serious endeavor of establishing a partnership, allocating a division of labor, and developing long-lasting habits. This usually covers a long period of time, may forecast permanency, and involves a merging of holdings, enmeshments of lifestyles and values, and the possibility of procreation. This stage can last as long as seven years.

The learned patterns that are developed during this stage establish continuity throughout the lifespan of the relationship. Couple's counseling and therapeutic intervention can be very effective and enhancing during this period when relationship patterns are being formed. Once patterns are set, they become habitual and considered the norm, strongly dictating modes of behavior. Intervention is always more difficult when long established habits are in place. With the passage of time, parties tend to become invested in holding on to even the most dysfunctional aspects of their behaviors. Psychotherapeutic intervention *before* habits take hold and solidify has a much greater likelihood of success.

Couples come together from varying backgrounds and lifestyles, each person carrying their own psychological baggage, expectations about love, hopes for the future, and notions of closeness and intimacy. During the "honeymoon period," the differences between participants in a dyad are obscure, and the possible conflicts unknown. During the "relationship period," however, the differences and conflicts are magnified and become obstacles to overcome. Guidance is often called for how to clarify common ground and discover give-and-take solutions. What usually occurs instead, though, is a series of power struggles.

An effective intervention is to have the couple describe their relationship challenges as a picture, asking that they visualize the differences that separate them from one another. The metaphoric images described by each of the two of them will show the ease and/or difficulty located within their conflicts. Examples of images that are often described include chasms, rivers, lakes, or mountain passes, with each party residing on the opposite "side" or bank.

Still using metaphors to describe and envision the separations between these patients, the therapeutic task is to discover whether or not the couple is able to find constructive ways to create connections and bridge these divisions. The goal is to see if the parties can imagine, through using the language of metaphors, a coming together and the development of some common ground that suits them both without conflict.

A very constructive and common sense image to introduce into this therapeutic process is **the bridge,** something that connects the division and builds a pathway. It is not a good idea to present the bridge metaphor, however, before asking the couple how they imagine making connections between the divisions, themselves. Although the idea of a bridge seems obvious, most couples struggle to find this way to connect the gaps. The bridge image comes more easily to couples that are more evolved and secure in their self-concepts.

By contrast, at first many couples generate images for making connections that involve *more* conflict, such as swimming across a river or body of water to reach the other side. Rowing in a boat is another popular suggestion for reaching the opposite side of the chasm, as are helicopters, planes, swinging on vines, and parachuting down.

When the patients' metaphors indicate that one member of the dyad has to abandon his or her side or territory in order to preserve the relationship and must move to the opposite side, there is not yet an equal place for give-and-take in the relationship. These types of images suggest that someone must sacrifice their own territory or place in life and move into the other person's world for the sake of the relationship.

In this scenario, one party would have to let go of whatever they had already built, while the other remained in their original territory. Traditionally it has been the obvious expectation that the female in a relationship would let go and move into the male's world. Today, however, this expectation is less obvious and much more complicated, bringing out an entirely new set of conflicts and negotiations.

When the members of a couple are stuck, struggling to find a method of crossing the chasm, the therapist can intervene and introduce the idea of building a bridge.

The bridge is a symbol for the creation of the relationship. What kind of a bridge it is, how it is built, what materials are used, and the time it takes to build it are all valuable diagnostic pieces of information that reflect on the struggle of the parties involved. As it is revealed, this information will aid the therapist in devising appropriate therapeutic tools, interventions, and solutions for his or her clients.

The aim of this exercise is for the couple to build a bridge together. It is comprised of the building blocks of their relationship. It is something unknown: a third territory, apart from each individual's own space. People come into any relationship with their own history and life experience. It is essential that each person have a strong, secure self-concept before they can be comfortable venturing out into unknown territory with someone else. Since creating this bridge is new territory, something unknown and insecure, the couple needs to be very confident and highly motivated in order to build their relationship.

A dance usually occurs when people first acknowledge the chasm between their two life experiences and then attempt to explore the possibilities of building a bridge. Most individuals are attached to who they are and are invested in their own particular views and beliefs. The first steps of the dance, then, involve persuading the other person to let them lead. If the pitch is successful, the leader achieves compliance from the other member of the couple and feels validated in the process. This achievement is temporary, however, and has negative consequences in the long run. The visual is two parties on either side of a bridge doing the "persuasion dance" as they try to woo the other to cross over and join them in their territory. This is a common initial maneuver.

The persuader is usually overly attached to their own values and self-concept, which may result in a need to compete or control, dominate, and win positions. If the other person is easily persuaded and crosses the bridge without asserting and clarifying his or her desires in the relationship first, a loss of self occurs, layered with doubt, blame, and anger. There is a sense of victory for the persuader, sure, but a no-win situation for the relationship itself.

If both parties duel, trying to win the other over to their side of the bridge, a power struggle ensues that can result in a battle and then the defeat of one party which can ultimately dissolve the marriage altogether. The therapeutic intervention is to emphasize the meaning of building a bridge as a *joint and equal venture,* with each step negotiated and agreed upon so as to encompass the needs and expectations of both parties. The goal is always to create a win-win solution. When two parties come together with all of their individual differences and expectations, a cohesive merger needs to occur, one that expands each person's territory into a third territory. If not, then the building blocks of the relationship are set on a precarious foundation, one that can lead to dissolution of the relationship.

The bridge represents the relationship that, in turn, is the third territory, one that is unknown and must be built by both participants in equal measure. The idea is for both people residing on opposite sides of the bridge to leave their territories and meet in the middle. Participants are advised not to abandon their own sense of self and all that has been built in their growth previous to the relationship. The ability to meet on the bridge tests the couple's "readiness" to be available for a partnership. If a person is secure within himself or herself, then being open to expansion and learning will be both positive and stimulating.

The therapeutic task is to assess the security and sense of self of each participant. Unfortunately, most people who come to couples therapy are disillusioned, angry, frustrated, and misunderstood. The communication between participants is often at a standstill. There is usually a struggle for power, and the winner believes that, by winning, their "rightness" is validated, and the other person is "in the wrong."

Building a Bridge

It is essential for the therapist to intervene *without taking sides or making judgments* about either party. The clarifications and reflections need to focus on the relationship and whether a coming together can be negotiated. The aim of the therapist is to show where the miscommunications are occurring that separate the couple from progress.

The bridge analogy effectively depicts the dynamic of the couple's experience at this juncture. The dysfunctional relationship contains many rips and tears; it is barely able to hold at the seams. It is as if the two people involved are each standing at the edge of an abyss, opposite one another; the gulf between them is dark, cloudy, and immensely vast. It occurs to neither one of them to build or find a bridge. Each individual wants the other person to prove their love and commitment to him or to her by coming to *their* side. It feels unsafe and scary to leave the stronghold on which they have made a stand. The gauntlet has been thrown down. Proof of love and commitment is demanded through their partner's sacrifice.

This scenario is set up to fail. If one partner wins, the other has to lose. A defeated partner carries resentment. Sacrifice is a double-edged sword. The winner can only win an alliance through mutual agreement. Otherwise, the battle may have been won, but the war has already been lost.

The art of therapy is to illuminate what is wanted in this transaction and to clarify the pros and cons of the demands. It is important to help the participants understand the consequences of their choices. Enforcing demands without considering their partner's needs and personal psychology is doomed to failure. If the objective is to preserve the relationship, then the therapeutic alternative is to help build a bridge.

The healing path for entrenched and dysfunctional couples is for them to create this "third territory" that respects and values each participant's individuality, including their existing beliefs and history. This third territory—their relationship—is built by both, toiling together in partnership in order to reach mutual agreement. It involves an *expansion beyond the individual sense of self* into an inclusion of the other. It also creates a merger that is new, and based on an ongoing building process that involves energy, hard work, respect, and, ultimately, love.

If the participants involved can view the bridge building as a metaphor for a constructive relationship, and then agree to embark on the process as equal partners in good faith, then the blueprint for a positive and sturdy structure will have been drawn. The tools for the developmental stages that follow are in place.

The bridge metaphor works best during the second stage of a relationship's development, before habits have solidified. However, its use has therapeutic value for individuals who want to come together at any stage of development to form a merger that will have longevity. The therapist can vary the metaphor and adapt it to suit any participants who are struggling.

ଔଔଔଔ

Case Study: Adam and Amy

The following case study describes how the bridge metaphor can be used and varied effectively in psychotherapy.

Adam was in his late forties. He had had two previous marriages and no children. He was in commercial real estate but felt that he was a misfit in that profession. He did triathlons, was a competitive swimmer, and loved to entertain the crowd with his humor and quick, sharp wit. He worked sporadically, saving just enough money to drop out and play for a while. He had numerous business ideas but hadn't pursued any of them seriously. He was a recovering alcoholic and had been clean for the last six years, although he did indulge in marijuana and occasional psychedelics. He attracted, and was attracted to, women much younger than himself.

Amy, a Japanese/American, was twenty-five years old when she first met Adam. She was a sweet, bright-eyed young woman. She worked as an event planner and traveled a good deal. She had never married and her last relationship had been with her boss. She still mourned her mother who had passed away from cancer four years before the onset of her relationship with Adam.

Adam and Amy met on a biking vacation. They literally bumped into each other as though providence directed their meeting. Conversation and attraction was immediate and mutual between them. Two years after meeting, they sought couple's counseling. They both appeared to be hurt, angry, misunderstood, and bewildered. The chasm between them was indeed wide.

At the time of psychotherapy, Adam was fifty. He was anxious to have children before it became too late for him to be a vibrant father. For the first time in his life he was conscious of his age. He wanted a mate who followed and adored him, and who saw him as her guiding light.

Amy, at twenty-seven, was a young professional who was devoted to her business and who wanted to expand. She was flexing her muscles in the world at that point, trying to discover her impact and strengths. She saw Adam as a teacher, especially in athletics; but she needed to find her own force and expertise. Following Adam had no appeal for her.

Adam was an early riser; Amy, a night owl who didn't function well in the mornings.

Adam liked to hold court. Amy wandered off and spoke to other men in ways that Adam found threatening. Amy had many ambitions that she hoped to fulfill. Adam wanted to settle down and make babies.

Adam assumed that all women wanted home, hearth, and children. Amy assumed that all men wanted adventure, experience, and fun. She was initially attracted to Adam's playfulness while Adam was attracted to Amy's youthful freshness and pliability. At this point in their relationship, both felt misunderstood and unloved by the other. Amy said, "If he loved me, he would know that I need to grow and evolve into the best I can be. My focus needs to be on myself." Adam said, "If she loved me, she would realize how important it is to have babies now and settle down before I get much older."

When their differences and wants became clear in therapy, they also realized that wanting different things out of life didn't have to cancel the love and strong feelings that they had for each other. The question became whether they could create and manage a venture that included *both* person's desires and hopes for the future. Would they be able to build a bridge that connected their wants into one large gestalt?

ରେଓେଓ

Psychological Dynamics

Adam and Amy mutually agreed that the image that best depicted the division and differences between them was that of two mountain peaks. Each person resided on his or her own mountaintop; valleys and steep drops separated them from one another. Adam saw a rope bridge connecting the two peaks. Amy saw the connection as an aerial tram, with two stations at each mountaintop.

They visualized the means of connecting their differences through this tram and rope bridge. They did *not* imagine building a connection as a joint venture. Also, Amy wanted Adam to cross over to her mountain peak and Adam wanted Amy to come to his side. Meeting in the middle did not seem like a safe option for either of them. Adam thought that it was possible to meet in the middle of the rope bridge, while Amy couldn't imagine herself on a rope bridge under any circumstances. It felt unsafe. She thought they could stop the tram in the middle of the mountains, but both concluded that the tram represented a confined, restricted territory for a merger, a space with nowhere to go. Their inability to visualize images that would connect their differences and make a new merger possible was telling in itself.

The obvious therapeutic intervention at this impasse was to suggest examples of mergers that could include both of their goals as well as present the blueprint for building a third territory called "the relationship."

It is best to construct concrete therapeutic examples based on the couple's own hopes and plans for the future. For instance, Amy had aspirations of attaining higher education. She wanted to study for a master's degree in a program that might involve moving to another state. If Adam agreed to the move and set up house, would she allow herself to get pregnant while she was attending school? This suggestion seemed unsatisfactory to both.

What became apparent, as other bridge-building options were explored, was that both Amy and Adam were more attached to what they wanted individually for themselves than they were to their desire to be with each other. Any proposed compromise felt like a sacrifice that demanded too much of one of them. In sadness, they looked closely at the option of parting company.

Neither Amy nor Adam was secure enough in himself or herself to be able to imagine moving outside of their individual self-concepts. Adam needed to come to terms with his aging process and settle down internally before he would be able to settle down with a partner. Amy had many lands to conquer and things to learn about herself, so settling down and becoming a mother focused on childrearing were not in her immediate forecast.

Each member of the couple made some weak attempts to persuade the other as to how attractive their individual side could be and what positive rewards joining them there could attain. The persuasion dance was half-hearted, however, and ultimately unconvincing. Both Amy and Adam realized that feeling love and attachment to each other was not enough to compel them to build a bridge and a life together.

CRCRCR

This case demonstrates how "the bridge" is an effective metaphor in helping dyads view their conflicts and struggles. The images generated by the participants are projections that at times defy conscious knowledge, but they can identify the issues quite clearly and get quickly to the heart of the matter.

CRCRCR

Veis Djalali

THE SIBLING CONNECTION

Siblings originate from the same gene pool. They incubate and grow into beings inside the same womb, are delivered through the same birth canal, are brought up more or less in the same environment and, presumably, by the same mother and father. These origins contribute to the creation of special and inherent bonds that are unique to and characteristic of sharing parents. Biological brothers and sisters have permanent connections, no matter what other circumstances arise in their lives.

Since these connections are a given, they are often taken for granted, but they reside in the consciousness as a sense of security. This is interesting, because the most pronounced sentiments expressed by siblings are rivalries, competition and rage. This love/hate connection has its ebbs and flows within any family's dynamics; it also correlates distinctly with any disproportionate attentions given by parents. Siblings complain about their parents' approval and favors, and sabotage one another's success. However, when attacked, either by parental displeasure and/or outside forces, siblings generally rally together, supporting and rescuing one another.

Boundaries regarding possessions can be murky between siblings. The secret sentiment expressed, as clearly observed in small children, indicates, "What is mine is mine, but what is yours I want and will take, if I can." The fights among siblings are mostly over possessions and their parents' favor. Old or young, sibling disputes reflect the struggle for entitlements and ownership. These are primitive feelings that we are taught to control and keep in check. As we grow and mature, the intensity of these feelings diminishes but returns in times of crisis.

The order and ages of siblings also play a significant role in the formation of these relationships and the overall family dynamic. There are a variety of general configurations that illustrate the sibling connections.

For example: The bigger the age difference, the lesser the likelihood for intense rivalries, and the greater the sense of protectiveness by the eldest sibling and hero worship by the youngest. If the first-born is a boy and the second child a girl, these children tend to grow up with the inherent understanding that males and females are different, have separate roles for behavior, and, therefore, expect different treatment. This configuration seems to generate less rivalry and more cooperation, unless the parents emphasize favoritism. If the first-born is a girl and the second child a boy, the son may grow up with feelings of inadequacy, since girls mature more quickly. The boy is always in second place and cannot ever really catch up with his sister until adulthood.

If the siblings are the same sex and close in age, the potential for rivalry and competition is highest. If there are many siblings (more than two), then hierarchies, alignments and partnerships develop. If there is one daughter in a group of two or more sons, the girl will adopt a role based on her parent's responses to being the only female child, and this will impact her relationships with her brothers. This is also true in reverse. If the parents revere their only son or daughter, jealousies and envy can dominate the sibling relationships.

The baby in a family seems to have a special place among all other family members. The baby is often more protected, petted, and made the object of the others' affections. Being the youngest in sibling birth order may inadvertently train the baby to develop unrealistic expectations of the world at large.

Being an only girl child among brothers may influence her to copy her brothers' behaviors and make them role models. An only boy child among sisters may grow up being spoiled, worshiped by his sisters, and consequently develop feelings of entitlement as regards all other relationships.

Usually the child who is most favored by parents is the most hated by his or her siblings.

Parents can form their own alignment with a particular child as well that communicates a disproportionate amount of attention to her or him and relative neglect to the other offspring. There are many other configurations and responses that occur; these form the foundation of most sibling dynamics. Of course, sibling relationships also evolve and change through life experiences, events, and demands.

Siblings, like other group constellations, develop roles that come to define their character, behavior, and place within the dynamic of various social structures. The parents' expectations and inevitable "labeling" that occurs through the processes of maturation are the major determinants of these roles, although formed unconsciously. Some examples of these labels and roles are: the "black sheep," the "good child," the "bad seed," the "caregiver," the "princess," the "spy," the "loony," the "fairy," the "taker," the "leader," the "brain," the "sensitive-one," the "manipulator," the "outlaw," the "jock," the "dummy," the "rescuer," and the "clown." These adopted and/or earned labels and roles are self-explanatory. They follow and determine an individual's behaviors throughout their lives. Psychotherapeutic interventions can often break these labels down and help to liberate patients so that they can reinvent themselves.

Often in times of crisis like an illness or the death of a parent, siblings are required to gather and make some necessary decisions. During these critical and emotional times, the originally formed dynamics within the siblings' relationships emerge and take over. Also, each sibling's individual relationship with his or her parents will be at play and will impact their evaluations and decision-making processes.

The cohesion and ability to make decisions collectively again depends on the kinds of roles and relationships that were formed within the family dynamic during their childhood years. The alignments, oppositions, and unresolved issues affect the group's ability to be cooperative and to achieve any kind of resolution. Sometimes the alignments that formed between siblings come into conflict with the relationships that they have with their parents. For example: in a time of crisis concerning the healthcare of a parent, a sibling may expect support from his or her brother or sister, and it may be withheld. This lack of support could occur not because of non-existent camaraderie between the siblings, but due to an old grudge or stored anger toward that parent. This will inevitably lead to conflicts between siblings.

The deaths of parents can inspire siblings either to draw closer or to dissolve their bonds entirely. When parents are no longer present, there are fewer reasons to clamor and compete for attention. As a result, siblings may begin to enjoy one another's company and express support more freely. On the other hand, the parents may have been the glue that held together the bonds between siblings. Once that glue is no longer present, the remaining bonds may not be strong enough to maintain a relationship between them.

Eventually, most siblings learn to develop their own individuality and achieve their own successes. They learn to be rivals and to compete yet to love and support one another. These dualities become both the strengths and possible downfalls in sibling relationships.

ଓଓଓ

Case Study: Arnold and Eric

The following case study describes some of the conflicts experienced among siblings.

The Sibling Connection

Arnold was the eldest son. His brother Eric was three years younger. There were also two sisters, an older sister who was married and had two children, and a baby sister who was still in school. They were first-generation Americans, the children of immigrant parents. Their father had retired from a family-owned business and designated Arnold to lead the business into the future in his stead. His brother Eric was to be second-in-command. The other stipulations were that Arnold provide for, and employ, the other siblings and their spouses in this family business.

Arnold was a visionary. He had grand ideas. He was also a good son, liked to please his father, and was fond of his siblings. Arnold felt confident, excited, and entitled to captain the venture of an enterprise.

Although Arnold had the heavy burden of being responsible for the family and everyone else who depended on him and his business acumen, he managed to bring the company up the ladder so that it realized substantial monetary gain and success.

Despite their squabbles, he and his brother Eric worked well together. Arnold was the idea man while Eric was good in sales. Eric, however, had ongoing objections about corporate expansion and grander-scale operations. He preferred small business and advocated downsizing.

All of the siblings were married eventually, had children, and were employed by the company in accordance with the conditions dictated by the father. Their spouses also held positions and collected salaries from the company. When the worldwide economic crunch hit, the company's revenues wavered. Everyone who had been so dependent and benefited so much fell into an uproar, voicing fears, concerns, and blame.

Arnold began to experience self-doubt. He was worried that his vision for continuous growth and expansion were no longer applicable given the current economy. The company was bread and butter for so many people that he became afraid of the consequences if he could not halt its downward economic trend. He also heard his clan expressing dissonance quite loudly.

Eric's notions of downsizing took on new significance. Eric felt validated by the economy's forecasts. He jumped on Arnold's self-doubt and campaigned ferociously for cuts, including the abandonment of larger projects. Eric vied for leadership. He wanted to take over and run the show. He was tired of following Arnold and playing second fiddle. He wanted to implement his own ideas, minimizing Arnold's control and removing him from the limelight.

Even though Arnold had provided well for his extended family, and his innovative ideas had guided the company into many successful ventures, he became filled with doubt and self-recrimination. He had believed that he and his brother Eric were on the same page, and that Eric liked and supported his leadership, so he was quite shocked by Eric's vehemence.

Up to that point, he had had no idea that Eric suffered in his role within the company and had long felt slighted by being in second position. Arnold had always assumed that he had everyone's support, as rightful heir to the family throne. Arnold also became aware that his sisters were resentful of his authority and of their dependence on him, regardless that they had always benefited from his bounty. It also became more evident that his brothers-in-law and sister-in-law were unhappy and wanted larger portions of the pie. Arnold had been under the illusion that he had been leading a happy ship.

The parents had been ill for a while. The father had had two open heart surgeries and the mother had dementia. Their influence and contributions to the family's decision-making processes were minimal and no longer sought.

Arnold's dilemma, in light of this new awareness, was how to regain his leadership position within both his family and his workplace. He had his own personal demons to overcome. He was both disillusioned and depressed about his family. He did not feel valued or believed that his hard work had been appreciated. He had also lost touch with the inspirational forces within himself. He wondered if he should abdicate and allow Eric to take over the company. He was afraid, however, that Eric might not have the vision and overall picture to run the company well. He worried that, with Eric at the helm, the company might soon lose its impact and influence in the marketplace. He acknowledged that Eric was an excellent salesman, but he believed Eric to be shortsighted.

ৠৠৠৠ

Psychological Dynamics

Before Arnold could review the duality of his role as head of a business and the primary breadwinner for his relatives, and contrast that to his personal needs as a family member, he had to find new meaning and inspiration within himself in order to rekindle his enthusiasm and inner spark. Arnold had to first become motivated once again, and lifted out of his depression and self-doubt. He was at his best when his inspiration and innovative ideas guided and directed him. Because he had lost touch with those inner forces, anxiety had overtaken his attitudes and self-regard.

Individual psychotherapy helped to restore Arnold's equilibrium and reconnect him to his natural resilience and creative talents. He was then in a better position to problem-solve the conflicts within his family and business. If his positive and resourceful attitudes could recover, he would be better able to choose the best direction to support his wellbeing and to also attain business success. If Arnold decided to assume the leadership position again with his inner fire intact, the lines between the business and the family could be explored constructively and new avenues discovered.

It is always difficult to mix business with personal concerns. For business matters, the main objectives are profit and gains. Transactions are cold and impersonal. With relationships between family and friends, much more caretaking and diplomacy is required. In a family-owned and family-operated business, the boundaries between the family's structure and the imposed demands of the business are often confused and in conflict.

Arnold was the leader of the family enterprise. He had not been elected to the job. It was his father who designated him as leader without any previous consultation or preemption. Arnold was comfortable assuming the responsibilities of leadership, but he had been under the illusion that the family members approved of and supported him as captain.

Arnold's need for his family to like and appreciate him operated on the personal realm, and interfered with his role as business leader. When he became aware of the discord and disdain expressed by his brother and sisters, he was hurt; this put his performance as leader of a corporation in jeopardy and compromised his feelings and self-confidence.

Therapeutic intervention helped him to clarify his priorities. He needed to sift through his own psychology and determine whether being liked had more value for him than being an effective leader and business entrepreneur. Usually, being liked and being successful and powerful are not in accord. Ultimately a choice has to be made, one that best suits a person's psychology. When Arnold was able to choose the avenue that best aligned with his priorities, his position and subsequent behavior also became clear.

Since Arnold was in business with his family members, he needed to wear different hats as the situation demanded. (Actually, it became essential for *everyone* in the family to learn this skill.) Arnold could not behave in a personal and vulnerable manner when he was conducting a business conference or making business decisions. People in hierarchical systems within any company often have objections to and responses against decisions that are made by those in power. This is the nature of corporate life.

When he was at functions with family members, it was appropriate to be personal and behave differently. At work, the structure changed, so Arnold had to learn to be objective; professionally, he could not be subject to his need for approval.

It became clear that it would be good politics to hold individual business meetings with his family members in order to negotiate and clarify the ground rules and expectations, as well as define each of their roles more explicitly. These meeting were designed to provide Arnold with the means to reassert himself once again as leader and to smooth some discord by adjusting the company structure based on the feedback that he gained.

The conflicts between Arnold and Eric were more complex, so they required more exploration. Obviously, Eric could no longer tolerate being in second position under Arnold's rule. The boundaries between being brothers and business partners had blurred and become loaded with pain. The strife between them had forced the other family members to choose sides, which furthered the disruptions and discord.

Arnold was the older brother and man in charge. Eric was having a hard time defining himself, separate from his reactions to Arnold as boss. Ideally, Eric could remove himself to an environment that was independent of his family dynamic and power positions; there, he could better discover himself and his needs. The likelihood of that, however, was minimal, given the high profits that Eric derived from the family business.

Another option was to explore whether a functional and cooperative business partnership could emerge between the brothers with new ground rules and better modes of communication. If this attempt failed, other possibilities to consider included:

> ➢ Could a separate position be created for Eric, giving him the total control over a section of the business? This position had to be independent from Arnold's rule and influence.
>
> ➢ Would the family be open to dividing the business assets so that each brother could own and head a portion of the company?
>
> ➢ Would a settlement of some sort satisfy the two brothers and dissipate the conflicts that had arisen given the confines of the partnership?

Exploring the options and their consequences was an exercise for the brothers to undertake, so that they could address to what extent they were willing to sacrifice assets in order to gain the choices that they preferred. This process would clarify the pros and cons and the losses and gains of the various options; then they could come to terms with their decisions and commitments. If there was a willingness to open the avenues to explore all of the various options, then there was a reasonable likelihood of finding a path that would be acceptable to both brothers.

As this case demonstrates, however, finding a mutually satisfying solution to sibling conflicts often involves considerable struggle between the parties, particularly when the stakes are high.

ଔଔଔଔ

FROM PROCREATION TO OLD AGE

As discussed in the previous essays, the first stage of a relationship is the initial attraction between two people, and that becomes the honeymoon period. The second stage is the struggle to form a relationship that has longevity and structure that ensures it has a future. Provided that a death, separation, or divorce does not occur within a relationship, the other significant stages that follow are:

- ✓ Procreation
- ✓ Child rearing
- ✓ Empty nest
- ✓ Retirement
- ✓ Old age, and
- ✓ Loss of partner to death

Procreation

When a dyad first expands its boundaries to include a third party, this stage is loosely termed **procreation**. Often the third party is a child. However, the significant inclusion need not be a child. Since the dynamics are similar, the inclusion can be a pet (usually the case with childless couples), a business project, caretaking of an elderly parent, or some designated venture like building a house.

The main characteristic of including a third party within the dyad is that it *needs the participation of both subjects* (willing or not) from its onset and then through development and maturation. The inclusion is a long-term project that requires care, time, vigilance, and work in order for important developments and growth to occur. A division of labor and planning are necessary for its care. The dyad needs to come together, and is forced to collaborate and share yet another responsibility. Previously the focus of the dyad has been on its own merging of goals and aspirations so that it was tuned to operate smoothly and benefited both participants. Once certain levels of comfort and ease are achieved within the merger, the dyad becomes psychologically ready to expand further and make room to include a third and significant focus.

ର୍ଥର୍ଥର୍ଥ

Case Study: Larry and Connie

The following case study depicts a heterosexual couple's developmental process toward the inclusion of children in their dynamic and illustrates some potential pitfalls that arise.

Larry and Connie were sweethearts in college. After dating for eight years, completing their post-graduate education and embarking on their individual professional paths, they decided to marry and formally set up house. Three years later, Connie became pregnant with their first child and four years later, they had their second son.

Connie came to therapy concerned about her relationship with Larry. He felt remote and distant to her. He shunned her efforts to reach him. The primary emotion he expressed was frustration over the clutter and mess that the children created. According to Connie, Larry seemed unreasonably angry toward their firstborn. She felt that he left everything for her to organize and coordinate. His participation in their lives seemed reluctant, perfunctory, and minimal. Since they both worked in high-powered positions, her load of chores at home felt disproportionate and unfair.

They rarely had sex and felt little desire for each other. Their lives at home revolved around the children and day-to-day life. Often the children slept in their bed, or Connie would fall asleep with one or the other of her sons while reading them a story. Their extended families were actively involved in their lives. They had Sunday dinners with their parents, and the grandparents took turns babysitting their grandchildren.

Larry spoke highly of Connie in terms of her devotion to the kids and her parenting abilities. However, he found her uninteresting as a woman. He said, "Our bed is not a marriage bed. It's one big cradle." She had nursed both children and was still "leaking milk," which was a turn-off to him. She wore ugly, utilitarian underwear and didn't seem aware of him as a man, never approaching him to have sex. She belonged to the kids and was always tired. He felt superfluous and unnecessary in his own home. He kept busy with outside activities, going to the gym regularly, playing basketball with friends one evening a week, and attending a writing class weekly. She felt that he took care of himself well and was self-centered, without caring that she might need a break and help around the house.

Soon after the initial therapy session, Connie discovered electronic exchanges indicating that Larry was in the midst of a love affair. When she confronted him, he confessed, but was unapologetic and had an air of self-entitlement. He professed that the affair had not become physical and promised to terminate the connection. He refused to discuss the matter further, however, and would not attend couple's counseling after that point.

Larry and Connie were of Latino origin. They had eight years of courtship before they married and lived together. They started their relationship at a young age, having had few previous experiences. Connie had been a virgin, and Larry had known only a few women before her. Prior to their children, Larry had Connie's sole focus. They traveled, entertained, and enjoyed each other's company. Their life was exclusive and fun. Larry was very excited at the prospect of fatherhood. Connie's first pregnancy brought them even closer, and they prepared together for the birth of their son.

When Tommy was born, however, everything changed. He mesmerized his mother, Connie. She wouldn't leave his side. She went from being a wife and active life partner to a wholehearted mother.

Larry couldn't find his place with mother and son. He was pushed into the background and felt that his wife's body belonged to his son while he had no rights to stand in their way. He devoted himself to work and was mostly absent. While Connie also continued to work, she felt abandoned by Larry and could not understand his aloofness and absence. She began to rely on him less and less. She breastfed Tommy until the age of three and only stopped because they decided to have another child.

With the birth of their second son, Brian, a routine had already been established. For the most part, Connie was in charge. During the week, she worked at her job and supervised childcare by grandparents and nannies. Larry was totally unavailable. Only on weekends did Connie, Larry, and their two sons have family time together. Sex between the couple was minimal and difficult to arrange. The focus was on the children or their work. Their relationship was unattended.

Anger and disappointment fueled many of the passive emotional exchanges that occurred between them. They had stopped talking to, and confiding in, each other. They were clueless about the other's feelings and struggles. The gap between them was growing.

They both adored their children and felt guilty if their focus on them wavered or became filtered by other considerations or "selfish" needs.

Larry felt depressed, resigned, and resentful. Connie was overworked and had no time for her or Larry. As with Tommy, she also breastfed Brian for the following three years.

Larry and Connie used to be close friends and talked about everything they felt and dreamed about. With the breakdown of communication between them, they grew further and further apart. Their conversations were about only the care and wellbeing of their children. It was as if, in the face of having children, their couplehood had no more importance. Their relationship had been neglected and was in a state of starvation.

Preserving the marriage and keeping their family intact did hold value for them both; yet Larry's betrayal and cheating seriously damaged the trust and its foundation. Connie could not imagine how to trust her husband ever again or even understand his behavior. She felt fooled. Larry's silence created a huge elephant in the room. He was determined not to make himself vulnerable to questions and accusations.

෬෬෬෬

Psychological Dynamics

This case is a classic example of what often happens when couples have children and become swept away by the demands of childcare and parenting. Therapeutic intervention entailed first educating the couple so that they could to see what had occurred when the dyad opened its boundaries to include a third and fourth party, and some of the consequences. The positive foundation within their relationship needed to be reinforced in order to remind the couple of their original attraction to each other and the initial choices they had made. What was difficult was trying to convince this couple that there were negative consequences to having given so much power and attention to their children at the expense of their relationship.

The structure of a well-functioning family must have a strong, united parent dyad at its head. This creates safety and positive boundaries for the children. The intense focus on children and lack of continuous communication between the couple were the obvious downfalls for this relationship.

Many steps could be taken to repair these tears. For example the marriage bed had to be reclaimed and sanctioned. The children had to be weaned from mother's breast and made accustomed to sleeping in their own beds. Mother had to take back her body and reconnect to the sexual being inside herself. Special time and occasions had to be set up for the couple to talk, share, communicate, and play without the presence of the children.

These efforts would help the couple to see the possible healing path to finding each other once again and paving the way toward closeness and interest. They would prove futile, however, if the wounds from Larry's betrayal were not addressed, and if moves toward reconciliation and forgiveness did not take place. It was likely that the extra-marital relationship was a symptom of the breakdown between the couple rather than a serious attempt to end their marriage. This needed to be assessed. The prognosis would become clearer as these attempts toward conciliations were made;

strong resistance to coming together would clarify the likely outcome of couple's therapy.

There is a power dynamic between this couple that might make progress slow, so it needed to be explored and opened up. While, on the surface, Connie appeared to be in charge of the family and home life, Larry held the power, and guided the main movements in their lives. Connie paid deference to her husband and Larry behaved entitled. Superficially they appeared to be a modern couple, both professionals, contributing equally to the life they had built. On closer scrutiny, however, strong traditional values were embedded in their individual psyches. This might have been causing confusion and stress in their judgments and expectations. Clarifying choices, roles, and the allocation of duties should shed light on this matter, and lead to the reassignment of more congruent boundaries.

The above case depicts what can occur when a couple that seems to have achieved ease and comfort in their dyad, could progress downward with procreation and the inclusion of children in their structure. This case exemplifies the need to be continuously aware and open to new learning and developing different tools in order to cope with the trials and tribulations of life.

At every juncture of development, there is potential for growth. However, the unknown can test the durability of any couple's commitment. How these tests are dealt with reflects the character, motivation, and ambitions of the relationship's strengths and weaknesses. What has been learned and what has worked in the past do not necessarily apply to the current demands. Couples need to be flexible and creative while maintaining openness. This is essential for the success of any relationship; this strategy will enhance their chances for survival in the face of any of life's many encounters.

ལ၈ལ၈

Child Rearing and Individuation

Ideally, the aim of most parents is to rear their children to become autonomous, independent, productive, healthy, successful, and happy individuals. Accomplishing this aim has layers of complexities. Generally, that sentiment does not rule the process. Rather, various unconscious, unresolved, and unknown psychological intents take control of parents' behavior and interactions. Also there are happenstances in life that are unpredictable and unexpected. The most that can be asked of any parent is that they do their best to instill in their children constructive survival and problem-solving tools that they can use to cope with the rest of their lives. A strong foundation instilled by parents allows children to grow and develop their abilities to face life on their own and to handle whatever cards are dealt to them.

There are stages to the process of parenting, each with its own unique demands.

When a child is first born, it is a helpless being, and totally dependent on others for its care and needs. The responsibility of having so much control over the welfare of a helpless child has profound impact on parents, and its own psychological dynamics. While they love the child, new parents still may feel overwhelmed, afraid of making mistakes, and resentful of having their life taken over by a speechless, howling infant. Parents can take to this process very naturally or they can have psychological issues that may hinder healthy interactions with their offspring. For example, some parents become too vigilant and overprotective in order to compensate for their fears and insecurities; others become negligent and even abusive, resenting the enormous responsibility that is required for an infant's care.

As the child grows from infancy and learns to walk, speak, and develop some limited independence, parents experience a mixture of positive and negative reactions. On one hand, they may experience some relief but at the same time develop separation anxieties. Up to this point, the child has had to be carried and under the total command of its parents. Now, the child has to be supervised closely and chased around as it develops a mind of its own.

When children start school and spend more and more time outside the family structure, being influenced and guided by other institutions, further separation anxieties can arise, along with fears of losing control. These anxieties are two-sided, both positive and negative, and may develop in both parents and child. How severe they are depends on how the experience is presented, viewed, and processed by all of the participants.

For example, toddlers often require a weaning period from their caregivers in order to be able to let go and become absorbed in their preschool and kindergarten activities. They may experience abandonment trauma if a parent leaves abruptly, and they are thrown into a school experience with no preamble. The parent, too, may feel a sense of loss and confusion when the intensity of care is less, becoming shared with outside facilities. The parent may also fear that what the child learns and experiences is no longer under his or her control.

Parents are, for the most part, heroes and the primary authority figures to their children until the age of nine or ten. However, in modern times and various cultures, this timetable may vary. The dynamic shifts completely starting with preteens and on into the teenage years. In healthy teenage development, it is appropriate for a teenager to question the value system and authority of his or her parents. During this period, the child learns to individuate and separate himself or herself from the parents, both physically and psychologically, in order to become an independent person.

However, this period is also fraught with danger and filled with behaviors linked to acting out; this tends to heighten emotions and create turmoil. The teenager is still a child with a brain not yet fully formed; nevertheless, she or he experiences a wide range of powerful emotions while stretching and reaching toward adulthood as though being on a rollercoaster ride. The teenager is in that twilight stage of not being a child and yet not being an adult.

Since the parents are no longer considered helpful authority figures, the teenager's primary guide becomes his or her peer group and circle of friends, comprised of young people who are also still children without fully formed brains. This sets up the potential for unforeseen dangers; the struggle can generate many disruptions within the family structure.

Most parents have difficulties with teenagers. They don't know how to be understanding while still maintaining some semblance of parental authority under the barrage of defiance and disrespect that is expressed by the teenager. It becomes a continual balancing act. There are parents who pride themselves on their parenting skills when their teenager does not rebel, behaves well, and is a docile child. Docile, cooperative behavior in a teenager is usually not a positive sign for this developmental stage. Some defiance is necessary to separate and develop autonomy.

Teenagers who never experience a rebellious period may carry a set of issues that can affect their entry to adulthood and maturity. There can be a number of reasons for this lack of rebellion linked primarily to the teenager's self-concept. For example, if a teen has a very domineering and/or punishing parent and does not have adequate strength built into his or her self-concept, it is too traumatic for them to rebel. It is also difficult to defy parents who are ill or who are especially sweet and gentle. A death or major catastrophe in the family can also result in a discontinuity during this developmental stage.

The passage from teenage to adulthood will occur eventually. What is required from parents is that they be strong in their values but judicious and fair. They need to model congruent, sensible, and compassionate behaviors consistently. The teen may appear oblivious or critical, but it will pay off in the long run.

ଔଔଔଔ

Case Study: Samantha and Henry

The following case study depicts a family that has difficulty allowing their children to individuate and become autonomous.

Samantha and Henry were African American. They met in college, then married and moved to Los Angeles. They were young, ambitious, and capable. Henry rose quickly in the television industry and became a major player. Samantha was also in show business and became a sought after casting director. There was a great deal of comradeship between the couple, and they accumulated wealth and success. The only fly in the ointment was that Henry drank "too much." With Samantha's urging and support, Henry joined AA, went cold turkey, and reformed completely.

Samantha stopped working when she became pregnant with her son, Robert; two years later, they also had a daughter, Karen. Samantha loved being a mother, and having children was very fulfilling for her life. The couple was enthralled with being parents, but some of the closeness between them diminished. The children took priority in their relationship, and their conversations were no longer about the adventures and events of work. The main focus between them became their children. Robert and Karen thrived; they seemed to be healthy, well adjusted, and intelligent, and doing very well in school.

As the children matured and became preteens, their body weight had been slowly increasing. In fact, all four members of the family—Samantha, Henry, Robert, and Karen—were overweight. Henry was the first in the family to raise the alarm. He joined Weight Watchers as the person most motivated to look good, being in a highly competitive workforce. Samantha followed suit but at a slower pace and had a harder struggle. The kids' weight, however, continued to increase into obesity.

Karen and Robert were both well behaved and did not express the "normal" teenage rebellion and disdain toward authority. They were high achievers in school and exhibited interests similar to their parents; they, too, hoped to join the show business industry. Henry, with his far-reaching influence, arranged internships for his children. Robert became an apprentice to a well-known film editor. He also loved writing stories. Karen apprenticed with a set designer, and her artistic inclinations flourished.

They did not make friends easily as their weight was a social deterrent at school. Both of them liked being at home with their mother and guided by their father. When the time came to pursue higher education, they opted to attend universities close by. Even though they lived in dormitories on campus, they came home every weekend.

The family structure remained intact until Karen became enamored with Stephanie and wanted to set up house with her. Samantha and Henry did not have any issues with their daughter's homosexuality. Both parents were open-minded and supported Karen's choice, however, her place at home became empty. Robert was then offered a job that took him out of the country. "Home" began to feel very empty for Samantha, so she was inspired to adopt two babies from Africa, convincing Henry to come on board. The little baby boy and girl were a joy. Samantha was in her element and once again deep in the throes of motherhood and caregiving.

The babies, Michael and Louise, were from different parents. Michael's learning disabilities were soon discovered and special education was set up for him early on. Louise appeared to be a "normal," happy child. Although slightly overweight, they grew quickly and adjusted well to school and surroundings.

Michael was docile and sweet, but Louise grew to be rebellious with no respect for authority. She formed "unsuitable" relationships with boys who were much older than she and started to spend very little time at home. Samantha had a hard time setting boundaries and ground rules for Louise. She was defiant and lied to cover up her misdemeanors.

Samantha and Henry were at a loss. It was difficult for them to impose harshness and discipline; they were much more comfortable just giving and providing. Louise's continuous rebellion and "outlaw" behavior baffled them.

At this juncture, the marital relationship between Samantha and Henry had also been slowly deteriorating, almost without their notice. Henry had had several romantic flings. Finally Samantha caught him in the act and filed for divorce. He made faint attempts to preserve the marriage but gave in to the divorce and a hefty settlement.

They were cool and distant at first but gradually developed a friendship and collaborated to parent their children. Eventually Henry developed a serious relationship with a makeup artist, and she moved in with him. Although Henry participated in family and social gatherings, his children and ex-wife ostracized Lizzie, the girlfriend.

Robert was protective of his mother and angry and unforgiving toward his father. He refused to acknowledge or recognize Lizzie. He moved back home with his mother and lived in an apartment above the garage. Robert had achieved some professional success but seemed to brood, becoming sullen and unapproachable. His supposedly temporary living arrangement above the garage dragged into years of complacency. Only Louise, "the outlaw," was able to make him laugh and remain close to him. Karen was worried about her brother. She confided to her mother her suspicion that Robert was abusing drugs.

Michael moved into an assisted living situation. He was able to do simple jobs to earn a little money and had a modicum of happiness.

Louise ran away from home and secretly married a felon who was on the run. She became pregnant, and then her husband was caught and jailed. She moved back home with her mother for care during her pregnancy. When Louise gave birth to a son, Samantha once again had a baby to take care of. She also assumed care for her drug addict son, Robert.

ଙଃଙଃଙଃ

Psychological Dynamics

Addiction to drugs, food, and alcohol was the major component of the dynamic in this affluent family. The addictions were not the root causes of the many dysfunctions, but they were the symptoms and coping mechanisms. The family structure reflected parents who were overinvolved with their children. They gave and provided for them to a crippling extent. The children, although intelligent and capable, hadn't been able to develop autonomy and independence. Their self-concepts regarding survival and inner strengths were weak and immature.

Samantha loved caregiving and defined her identity in terms of motherhood. When she wasn't serving in that capacity, she lost her sense of self and life's direction. Henry conducted, provided, problem-solved, and arranged life for his children. He was very good at it, so the children all became dependent on their father to make everything work well and to open opportunities for them.

Robert was very unhappy and undefined. He could never measure up to his father's stature. He glorified this parent yet hated him because of his own failure to do better; that explained why he numbed himself with drugs and food. His source of strength had become his anger. He found one way to separate from his father by taking his mother's side. He still resisted becoming his own person and remained in reactive, teenage mode. Even though he was over forty years old, he was obese, jobless, and without a significant other.

Karen perpetuated and continued the "mother" dynamic. She was in a relationship with Stephanie, who was both mother and father to her. They had three adopted children. Like Karen's father, Stephanie was an excellent provider. They were a very insular couple. Karen often found herself torn between her allegiance to her mother and to Stephanie. Samantha was an active grandmother, but in contrast to her parenting style, Stephanie and Karen imposed strict boundaries. Clearly, without Stephanie, Karen would not have been able to withstand the domination of her parents.

Michael had separated from the family's dynamic due to his learning disabilities. His role in the family was similar to that of a pet: he was loved, indulged, and cared for, but he lived on the fringes of the structure.

Louise was an outlaw: manipulative and self-serving. She didn't want to let go of the many benefits provided by Henry and Samantha, but she also wanted her freedom. She played at both ends but hadn't developed the strength to stand on her own. Like Robert, she remained stuck in the teenage life stage, reactive and acting out, even though she was twenty-five years old and a mother herself.

Each family member replayed his or her very same roles; this seemed to maintain equilibrium and perpetuate the status quo. Any change was experienced as a threat. Even though Henry and Samantha were divorced and Henry lived with another woman, their relationship to each other had remained solid and primary through their parenting. Their children had all made attempts to "leave home" and achieve individuation but had not been successful.

Robert left home for work but was always guided by his father's influence. He had been unable to grow his own wings. He indulged in drugs and food to numb his pain and keep him from facing his feelings of failure and self-hate. Karen recreated her family's dynamic with Stephanie and replicated her mother's persona. She was a devoted mother to her girls and loved caregiving. Her identity was enmeshed first with her mother and father and then with Stephanie. Michael, because of his disabilities, was not in the position to ever leave home completely. Louise only played at being her own person, remaining totally dependent on her mother's care for her baby; she continued to party without any particular direction for her life.

An initial family therapy session was useful in order to distinguish collectively how each member played a role in the family's interactions. It also helped to identify the covert and overt rules to which the family adhered in order to preserve and perpetuate status quo. After that, each family member needed individual therapy in order to separate them therapeutically, and to assist in the development of stronger senses of self; each one needed to become autonomous from the other family members. Robert was the designated "patient" in this family system. He represented the wounds and sorrows of the family's inability to escape from the enmeshed structure. The mother, Samantha, was the nucleus of this family. All of the other members revolved around her care and good will.

The goals of therapy were to rebuild the self-concept of each member so that they became strong, confident, and separate individuals, able to standalone without losing their sense of family.

There were plenty of talents in this family mixture, along with intelligence, caring, and the means to create a positive outcome.

ભ્રભ્રભ્ર

Leaving Home/Empty Nest

Around the age of eighteen or nineteen, the child has emerged into adulthood. The dynamic between parent and offspring shifts again. This is normally a "leaving home and empty nest" period. The child goes away to college, takes a separate dwelling and/or gets married. Although the generation gap between parents and their adult children is still obviously present when they are this age, the defiance and disdain of the teenage years has diminished. Hopefully the young adult is ready to leave the roost, having gained the appropriate tools to face life on his or her own.

Going to college and living away from home are experiences that test out the abilities learned by the young adult. Home and parents are still within reach, to check in when needed or have a place to rest and recharge when wounded. There are young adults who are not able to leave home at this developmental stage. They may not have the strength or confidence to do so, or the family dynamic may make it too difficult for them to leave. Also, in these modern times, children have been forced to move back home for economic reasons, since the job market has become so unpredictable and restricted.

Parents also have developmental issues to deal with at this juncture. They experience an existential crisis. Their identities have been firmly embedded in parenthood for eighteen years or longer, depending on the number of children they have had. With their children leaving the nest, parents have to redefine themselves and rethink their priorities and responsibilities, along with how they have been living their lives. Sometimes the degree of anxiety felt at this juncture is so extreme that any positive growth and rediscovery is not yet possible. To avoid the disruption, some parents produce *new* offspring or adopt children in order to start the childrearing years all over again.

More positively, some go back to school to resume a degree that they were not previously able to accomplish. Others start new businesses and projects, and even dabble in the creative arts. This is a period full of possibilities and potential for rediscovery and growth. Whether this opportunity is managed well and directed positively depends a great deal on a well-balanced attitude, and if the motivation to have a productive life that gives meaning and generates new direction exists in the individual's repertoire.

Another dynamic that faces the empty nest is that the family is reduced to its original dyad. "Couplehood" needs to re-form and rediscover its boundaries and connections. This process can be positive or negative, depending on the solidity of the relationship. Some couples have stayed together only for the sake of the children, keeping the family intact during the childrearing period. Once the nest becomes empty of offspring, permission to leave might be assumed by one participant or another.

Sometimes couples have grown apart and developed conflicting interests. When the focus comes back to them, the priorities in their relationship also shift. How they will reconnect with each other without the presence of the children is something to examine. They may discover that the distance and the discrepancies between them are too glaring and irreparable.

On the other hand, couples may benefit from being freed from the demands of constant care, gaining the time needed to become even closer to each other and to develop new bonds and interests. Couples need to get to know each other again and reevaluate the quality and direction of their lives from this new perspective. Their children no longer dominate and dictate their priorities. It is a period for renewal. Whether it is interpreted as such becomes the question.

Couples experience the redefinition of their roles and connection during several significant periods in the cycle of life. They redefine themselves when they first come together. They discover new aspect of their relationship and their own capabilities when they become parents. Then their relationship is retested when their children leave home, and again when they retire from their professions.

ଓଓଓ

Case Study: Ricardo and Maria

The following case study describes a couple who stayed together primarily for the sake of keeping the family intact as their children grew to maturity. The struggle to work through unresolved, postponed, and unforgiving issues from their past determined if the desire for renewal and continuation of their marriage still existed for them both.

Ricardo and Maria knew each other from childhood, and married when they were still in their teens. They were distant cousins. Their families were close socially and were pleased with the nuptials. Both Ricardo and Maria were attached to their family of origin and relatives. However, they moved to another state for work and became separated from their extended families. They only had each other in this new environment. Neither person had had many previous romantic experiences. But they were in love and excited about building a life and family together. They both worked and accumulated comfortable wealth. They had two daughters. Their marital relationship seemed to be satisfactory. However, their ideas about lifestyle, entertainment, and childrearing were markedly different.

Maria was very social and enjoyed entertaining and attending musical and theatrical events. Ricardo was reluctant to go to parties and socialize with Maria's friends. He liked to play poker with his buddies and have an occasional night out with them. He didn't enjoy talking or sharing. He didn't appear that involved with raising his daughters, either. He focused primarily on business and work. When he came home from work, he would have a drink, watch some TV, and then retire to his garage/workshop or play on the computer until bedtime. This distant, self-absorbed behavior infuriated Maria. She felt he was not her partner and did not love or appreciate her. She wanted his attention to be on her. She needed his help with household chores and the parenting of their daughters.

When the children were in junior high school, Ricardo had to travel for business for three months. While away, Maria heard through the grapevine that he had "shacked-up" with a very pretty blonde woman. Discovering the address, Maria showed up on their doorstep, unannounced. She saw for herself that the rumors were true. Ricardo had fallen madly in love with a Scandinavian woman. He was in anguish. He claimed to love his family deeply but could not leave Greta. Maria wanted nothing to do with him. His behavior and unfaithfulness were unforgivable to her.

It took two years for Ricardo to "come to his senses": to leave Greta, win back Maria, and come home. Maria relented for the sake of the children but did not trust or forgive her husband's indiscretion. Ricardo could not regain the passion he had for Maria or transfer the intensity he felt for Greta to his wife. His guilt and sense of responsibility toward his children persuaded him to sacrifice his feelings for Greta and to "do the right thing." Maria's heart had been shattered. She could not forget the image of the blonde woman. She even dyed her own hair blonde and attempted to be sexier for Ricardo. But the betrayal and belief that she did not fully dominate her husband's heart never left her. She saw herself as the second fiddle and a moral obligation; that was unbearable to her. But, like her husband, she was committed to keeping the family intact for her daughters.

Life went on. Their daughters matured and left home for college. The nest is then empty. Ricardo and Maria had no more excuses to be together. They had to face each other and their disillusionment. All of the years spent on pretense and moral righteousness could not heal the deep wounds that each had sustained. The pain of betrayal and loss rushed to the forefront once their nest became empty.

CRCRCR

Psychological Dynamics

Maria and Ricardo rationalized their reconciliation after the infidelity episode as a "grand sacrifice" for the sake of their children. Maria could not forgive Ricardo. Her "sacrifice" was to learn to live with him, despite her broken heart and lack of trust. Ricardo felt resigned, like he was settling not because he wanted to but because he *had* to, to be a "good person." He sacrificed his love of Greta.

Neither Maria nor Ricardo had fully considered in any depth what the "sacrifice" entailed. They merely implemented coming back together as their grand gesture. They had not understood, much less admitted, that choosing to stay together may have had an inner purpose, loaded with psychological complexities and self-centered needs. The righteousness of the "sacrifice" created an attractive and superficial explanation for keeping their marriage and family intact. However, this mode of being together permitted them to remain superficial, and it limited their ability to be more intimate and close with each other.

In the initial phase of psychotherapy, this unconscious collusion of adhering to the "sacrifice" stood out as the obvious place for intervention. How it was that the couple collaborated to maintain only minimal degrees of closeness needed to be explored. The therapeutic inquiry was to examine the personal intentions that drove each person to curtail the development of intimacy. They both had opportunities for a different life, yet they chose *this* one, and labeled it a worthy "sacrifice" that they would live by. Ricardo could have left Maria and experienced his grand love with Greta. Once divorced, Maria could have had other opportunities and prospects—she was a beautiful, accomplished woman. They could have entered marriage counseling at the initial point of crisis in their lives. Psychotherapy could have helped them learn to forgive and rekindle their love and closeness. Yet instead, they seemed to draw some gratification from remaining together but being sullen, angry, and withdrawn. The psychology behind this choice for martyrdom was important to clarify.

When the children left for college, Maria and Ricardo were only in their mid-forties. Still young and attractive, they were both faced with the choice of leaving the marriage to discover more meaningful relationships and self-fulfillments, but they were ambivalent and unsure of their next steps. The "sacrifice" that had been the glue holding them together was no longer applicable. Discovering what other positive values their lives together embodied, apart from the "sacrifice," was another goal for psychotherapy.

One of the most positive attributes reflected in this union was their long history of knowing each other: they were relatives; their families interacted from childhood; and they grew up together. Despite marked personality differences, they had been habitually comfortable with each other to the point of complacency. They seemed to fear challenges. They operated in the realm of minimal effort, even if the consequences limited their personal gratification. They clearly had the opportunity to forgive the past, renew their marriage contract, and achieve more closeness. The question, however, was, "Did they want to?"

Some of their ambivalence stemmed from a lack of experience on both sides. Life had not tested their capabilities as individuals in order for them to develop independent strengths. They married when they were very young, and their union became a protective shield. When Ricardo's transgression moved him out from under "the shield," life became too scary. Preserving "the shield" was this couple's main motivation for being together. More intimacy between them was interpreted as placing "the shield" in jeopardy, as well. Strong feelings and expectations were unknown and uncomfortable factors, and could therefore crack "the shield." They lived by that "logic" in covert agreement.

A temporary, therapeutic separation was advisable for this couple; the stress of being apart had to be monitored so that it did not become too extreme. They needed to grow, independent of each other, and become strong within themselves before they would be able to choose being married, whether to each other or to other people. Individual therapy helped them discover identities separate from their union. Once they became comfortable in their independence and autonomy, they could make other decisions with balance and fortitude.

The separation had to be designed and structured to suit the needs of this couple for maximum therapeutic benefit. Six months to a year was the designated period, after which they could evaluate their progress. Ground rules and codes for behavior and interactions were set for the duration of the separation. The length of their time apart depended on how

Ricardo and Maria evolved and processed their growth. When the timing was appropriate, they came back together to decide the direction of their future. There were still choices. Would it be with each other? Divorced? Or would they need an extension of the separation, in order to further self-explore?

ભઉભઉ

Retirement

When adults mature and progress in their professions toward retirement, more psychological shifts take place. Prior to retirement, the concept of "home" is generally one of a family center and sanctuary from business and the outside world. "Home" has meant a safe place to rest and recharge, free from the routines and demands of work. In modern times, however, given the age of computers, home has evolved into a convenient place for work, as well. This has brought changes and new complexities to the concepts of home and of retirement. So, for our purposes, home becomes "home" when the computer activities related to work are turned off.

Some people don't have set hours for work when they are at home, however. The boundaries separating "work" from "home" do not apply to this group. For them, their house is the primary place in life. Their relief from work is taken whenever they are involved in other activities or go outside of the house. For people who work from home, retirement has come to involve a unique set of boundaries. The longevity of continuing to work from home depends on its demands and the potential for conducting business lucratively.

When either or both participants in a dyad retire, the concept of home as a place of rest also changes. Home becomes the primary place to be, as regards to the quality and quantity of their time. Whatever or wherever home is, it must contain adequate stimulation to occupy and interest its inhabitants, fulltime. Affluent people travel a good deal during this period. They buy vacation homes and renovate them in order to provide additional stimulation within their environment. Often, gardens are created and patios and decks are built. Some people join golf and yacht clubs, and enlarge the circle of their acquaintance. The aim of these retirees is to fill the gap that work hours used to occupy. At the outset of retirement, there may be a frenzy of activity; alternately, some people experience a depressed and deflated period.

People who have been married to their professions find retirement more arduous; it is particularly difficult for them to bear the complete halt of their habitual routines. People who tend to be reactors and externally guided also experience anxiety when the external directives of work are no longer present. By contrast, people who are internally motivated and who generally have an abundance of ideas and wishes to fulfill, make their retirement period productive, positive, and even fun.

The psychological dynamics present at this point in life revolve around the retiree's internal struggle to redefine his or her needs and to plan new directions to take. Also, the retiree's interactions with a spouse who has resided at home usually undergo major changes and readjustments. The spouse who has not worked outside of "home" may feel that his or her space is invaded by the fulltime presence of the now-retired partner.

In order to ensure harmony and cohabitation, a couple needs to consider many changes. Notions of privacy, space and "alone time" take on crucial new meanings. Both participants had plenty of privacy and space when one party worked outside of "home." Upon retirement, the couple is in each other's constant company and oftentimes underfoot. Rearranging the space at home to allow for some privacy and independence from each other is advisable for soothing this transition. Simple reconfigurations make big differences in establishing comfort. If the basic foundation of a marriage is sound, and when a couple is committed to working together, then, with patience and due diligence, this transition should be positive.

ஐஐஐ

Case Study: Frank and Sylvia

The following case describes a couple that has different notions regarding retirement.

Frank and Sylvia have been married for twenty-three years. He is seventy-two and this is his third marriage. Sylvia is sixty-five and it is her second marriage. They both have grown children and grandchildren from previous spouses, although neither of them is close to any of their offspring. Their circle of friends is casual.

Sylvia worked as a medical receptionist and had been retired for five years. Frank was an entrepreneur/developer who purchased land and then constructed and sold houses. He traveled a good deal and was rarely at home. His mindset did not anticipate retirement any time soon. His success and wealth were revitalizing to him. Sylvia, on the other hand, had been waiting impatiently for Frank to retire and then move to Tuscany, Italy with her. She was fluent in Italian and had always dreamed of living there. She wanted to fulfill this dream before they grew much older.

Frank loved making money. He couldn't imagine doing anything that would entertain him as much or give him more gratification. Retirement felt like a death sentence to him. He operated under a high degree of tension as he wheeled and dealed. He drove a fast sports car and conducted many of his transactions on the phone while in transit. Unlike his wife, he found the idea of a sedate, pastoral life in Tuscany quite farfetched. He felt that he had already made his lifestyle concession when he gave up his beloved New York City and moved to Los Angeles to please his wife.

Sylvia could not reconcile herself to living as they had been, just for Frank's sake. Although she lived in a lovely house and spent her days with friends, engaging in fitness and healthy pursuits, her aspiration to live in Italy had become an obsession.

The situation was set up as "win or lose" for both parties. Their personal forecasts into the near future were completely different. If Frank gave up his business and moved to Italy for Sylvia, he had to condemn himself to a life that held no interest for him. If Sylvia relented and gave up on Tuscany, she would lose the dream of her life.

ଡ଼ଡ଼ଡ଼

Psychological Dynamic

The therapeutic intervention here was to first clarify the priorities and importance of this couple's values. They needed to acknowledge to themselves and to each other what had priority. Was the decision to live and work together more or less important than their lifestyle choice? If *being together* for the rest of their lives were a priority for both partners, then they would be open to finding an alternate path together that suited both their needs to some extent. If their *lifestyle* was more important, then the couple had to come to terms with that reality and make choices accordingly. The "building a bridge" metaphor (as described previously) was a logical tool for this sort of decision-making process.

Fortunately or unfortunately, matters were taken to a different level when the economy crashed, strongly affecting the housing market. Frank's lucrative business suffered major losses, and he had to shift his focus to salvaging his company and making the best deals possible under the circumstances.

The decision to move out of the country became more palatable for Frank; unfortunately, a move to the Tuscan countryside was not an option that he could embrace. This was the first time, however, that he made an initial step toward Sylvia's notion of retiring to foreign shores and gave it serious consideration. Which location would suit both their needs had to be negotiated. In therapy, to guide the process, the principle ground rule set for this negotiation was, "There can be no winner or loser in this quest."

Sylvia's eye was on Italy since she spoke fluent Italian; her obsession about the Tuscan countryside specifically, however, softened when Frank became receptive to the idea of moving abroad. Frank was inclined toward London or Sydney, since he only spoke English and could not imagine himself anywhere but in a major cosmopolitan city. The couple implied that the choice to remain together was a primary priority, even though it was never explicitly expressed. On some level, they enjoyed the struggle of trying to sell and persuade the other on the merits of various locations during their exploration. The depth of their differences was covered up by a playful, teasing banter.

The final decision was to take a year off and explore various options in search of a retirement location. The task was for each person to pinpoint five places that interested him or her. The plan entailed using the year to visit and assess those ten locations together and to narrow their final choice to the one place that best suited both of their needs.

At the end of the year of traveling and experiencing firsthand the realities of the various locales, hopefully they would create a cooperative joint venture and take a mutual decision that pleased both parties.

ୠଔଔୠ

Grandparents

The period of retirement usually coincides with grandparenthood. However, depending on the ages of all concerned, it's possible to become a grandparent as early as age forty. Whenever the first grandchild is born, a couple's identity and self-concept shifts and expands from being parents to becoming grandparents, as well. How people view themselves when they become grandparents can be a double-edged sword. On one level, the finiteness of life, the imminent passage of time, and eventual death become more apparent and tangible. The life cycle clearly presents itself when your children have their own children. On another level, however, the awe and sweetness of the event seems to create an instant bond between grandparent and grandchild. This phenomenon has been profusely depicted in literature.

At this juncture, the family expands to make room for the new offspring and whatever the new generation entails. Grandparents are elevated to the honored position of "elder" in the family structure. Boundaries for who dominates the parenting directives for the grandchild may be confusing for some people. While the actual parents are the rightful guardians of their children, the role of grandparents in childrearing has to be clearly defined and implemented. Grandparents may assume that they know best and that they have the right to advise and interfere in their grandchild's upbringing. These are issues for potential conflict between parents and grandparents who remain enmeshed and who have not experienced healthy transitions in their growth and maturation stages. It is very difficult to become a partner and/or a parent if "leaving home" has not yet occurred, in the full psychological sense. An autonomous and independent self-concept allows new parents to invite and implement help without blurring the boundaries around who is in charge of a new grandchild.

There are grandparents who are busy pursuing their own interests and so are absent from their grandchildren's lives; there are other grandparents who are involved and active in raising and guiding the new offspring. In modern times, when parents both work in fulltime positions, grandparents are often invited—in fact, expected—to chip-in as babysitters. This may be out of necessity, but it invites some grandparents to be more involved than is comfortable; conflicts around interference develop. The generation gap between parents and grandparents in terms of values and styles of caregiving can also create problems. Close involvement by the in-laws and the power dynamics that sometimes ensue can also generate anxiety and discord.

Children, by and large, are fond of their grandparents. Grandparents enjoy connecting with the new generation, and often express warmth and affection more freely than they did when they had the burden of full responsibility for raising their own children. In essence, while parents do the primary work of childrearing, grandparents can have fun, enjoy, and play with the new offspring.

Families that work and function well together incorporate an effective balance in their involvement and interactions with one another. The notion of *good balance* involves many things. Grandparents who have activities and a life of their own, separate and apart from their children and grandchildren, are in a stronger position to fulfill their role as grandparents. If their focus is primarily on rearing their grandchildren, then the balance is off. Over-involvement operates as over-compensation when there is lack of self-direction. These grandparents have not adjusted well to their aging process and this specific developmental life stage.

If the parents of new offspring are still enmeshed with their family of origin and did not "leave home" appropriately, their own needs and insecurities will prevent proper bonding with their spouse. The balance of their allegiance and priorities is confused. They live life with one foot in their own house and another in their parents' house. Unable to establish and develop their own clear boundaries and limits, they need to consult, seek advice, and solicit help from their family of origin. If overdone, it eventually will bring about a breakdown in the couple's relationship.

A complete lack of involvement between grandparents, parents, and grandchildren poses its own set of problems. It is healthy and rewarding for familial generations to care for, interact with, and plan activities around one another. When boundaries are intact and healthy developmental stages have transpired, fruitful and memorable interactions can be anticipated. Family enjoyment is at its best when it is not based on need, but instead celebrates family and bonding.

ଔଔଔ

Case Study: Lillian and Amber

The following case study describes a family that had difficulty with setting appropriate boundaries as they defined the roles and relationships of parents, grandparent, and child.

Lillian became a grandmother at the age of fifty-two. Her only daughter, Amber, lived in another city and gave birth to her grandson, Kyle. She fell in love with the baby boy on sight. She wanted to be near her grandson and helpful to her daughter, so she moved to the town where her daughter and family resided. Amber worked full time and planned to return to her job a few months after giving birth. After much discussion and debate, it was mutually agreed that Lillian would move in to her daughter's house. She got along well with her son-in-law, Kevin; they were fond of each other and did not anticipate having conflicts of interest.

Lillian divorced her husband, Steven (Amber's father) when she was still a young woman. She did not remarry, but

Steven did, and had a new family in another state. He rarely saw or interacted with Amber.

After the divorce, Lillian moved with Amber to the house where she grew up, in order to live with her mother. The three females lived together throughout the early years of Amber's life. Amber grew very close to her grandmother, Eloise, who became a significant role model. Eloise was the matriarch and exuded charisma and influence.

The three generations—grandmother, mother, and daughter—lived together for many years in solid union, with grandmother as the head of the family, mother Lillian as a passive subordinate, and Amber as the princess.

Eventually, Amber moved away to attend college, and while at school, her grandmother passed away. Lillian was left alone and without an anchor, since her family had suddenly dissolved. Her work took on new importance in her life. She was the assistant to a high-powered politician; she achieved a certain amount of independence and was able to take care of herself. Some years later, Amber married and announced the birth of Lillian's new grandson.

In order to relocate to be with her daughter's family, Lillian had to give up her job and the life she had built for herself. She basically assumed the role of live-in nanny. Amber became more involved in her profession, and she became more dependent on Lillian's care for her son Kyle and the management of household matters. Though grateful, Amber also resented the growing closeness between her son and mother. She was angry and autocratic when at home, finding fault with Lillian's arrangements. They often argued and raised their voices. Lillian adored Kyle and wanted to be with him all the time. She did not like being around her daughter and her "tantrums." She thought that Amber was a negligent mother and an unworthy wife to her son-in-law, Kevin.

Amber had idealized the notion of having her mother live with them and being a grandmother to her son. Since her experiences with her own grandmother were so memorable and significant, she wanted to recreate that for her son. Having her mother live under the same roof became problematic, however. She felt she was losing her role in the family, with her mother usurping her position. Her inclination was to kick her mother out of the household and limit her ability to interact with her son.

How to accomplish this decision and not cause undue trauma and guilt were the questions to explore in therapy.

CRCRCR

Psychological Dynamics

This case is a glaring example of how relationship history and unresolved issues repeat themselves within a family's dynamic and are often passed on to a new generation. The influence of the family's matriarch, Eloise, was a domineering force that shaped the values, beliefs, and behaviors of Lillian and Amber.

Lillian never "left home" psychologically, so she wasn't able to bond with her husband, Amber's father. After a brief interlude with him, she moved back to live in her mother's shadow and under her rule. She relinquished her place and responsibility as mother to Amber, in essence allowing Eloise to replace her. This replacement did not seem inappropriate to her at the time. She had accepted that Eloise was the ruler and her own role was subordinate. She believed that this was best for all.

Amber grew up feeling that the universe revolved around her and her needs. She was secure in the single-minded and self-centeredness of a child who is entitled and privileged.

When Eloise died and Amber was away in college, a window of opportunity slid open for Lillian to grow and find strength and independence. Unfortunately, upon the birth of her grandson, the "old" family values burst forth and guided her behavior. Almost unconsciously, she replicated her mother's position in the family structure. She was compelled to take charge by supplanting her daughter and becoming the matriarch.

Amber's personality, however, was not the same as Lillian's when she was a young mother. Amber was not meek or subordinate. In fact, she had upgraded herself from princess to queen. She liked to use her mother's help for the benefit of her family, but she would not tolerate her mother taking over and replacing her. She was *also* driven to be the matriarch like her grandmother. Mother and daughter became rivals for that position.

Conjoint therapy with mother and daughter had initial benefits to help them become aware of their history, their psychological development, and the significant role that Eloise played in shaping their thinking and expectations. Both Amber and Lillian needed to "leave home" in the psychological sense and distinguish their personalities from Eloise. They needed to identify their own individuality and separateness, and embrace it. Also, it was significant that they reconnect as mother and daughter, since this connection was never well established. The emphasis was to restore Lillian as Amber's mother, not Kyle's, and to clarify that Eloise was Lillian's mother, not Amber's.

Lillian's relationship with her mother, Eloise, was ambiguous. Although she had grown up dependent on, overly attached to, and intimidated by her mother, there had been no fondness or closeness between them. Lillian was at a loss as to how to be a "mother" to Amber, who was already a grown woman who could take care of herself. Eloise overshadowed Lillian to such a degree that Amber grew up dismissing her mother and not respecting her as a presence. She modeled herself in her grandmother's image. Her mother had been a doormat in her mind, not a person of interest.

In trying to take over her daughter's household, Lillian showed to Amber some gumption and personality for the first time. She had become a worthy opponent.

Getting mother and daughter to know and recognize each other from a fresh perspective was material for therapeutic intervention. Exploring avenues of viewing one another as grownups, and apart from Eloise's shadow, presented the opportunity to test whether or not there were ways for them to connect on a positive level. Opportunities to like and/or respect one another would follow. If Lillian was able to learn to be a mother to Amber, then her perspective could change, allowing her to learn to be a better grandmother to Kyle in the process.

ଓଓଓ

Old Age

It is interesting that the end stage of life is referred to as the "golden years." Hopefully "golden" refers to an attitude rather than to the physical aspects of aging. The ability to have positive attitudes and resilience and still embody a zest for life determines the type of aging process that a particular individual will experience.

Aging is a difficult period for most. It is the longest developmental stage. In the stage of childhood, the compass heading points toward growth, maturation, and the acquisition of new strengths and abilities. The view toward the future is glorious with possibilities. In adulthood, the shortest developmental stage, fulfillment of growth attained is experienced and enjoyed. Old age poses the diminishment and loss of the body primarily, plus sometimes of the mind. The compass needle points toward death. When faced with illness, chronic pain, and disabilities, maintaining a positive and accepting attitude becomes of paramount importance. Elderly couples that take care of and support each other are in stronger positions to cope than are couples that become resentful of aging and who fight the inevitable.

Psychotherapy can aid the elderly to face the transition to old age with acceptance and a measure of pragmatic forbearance. It is wise to consider the possible outcomes of aging, to explore choices and make provisions while a person is still fully able. "Trust" in caretakers and institutions become a major factor as the elderly person begins to lose control of their self and body.

This loss of control over life choices can be devastating. Depression and anxiety are prevalent psychological conditions during this period. It is important to have someone—a child or relative—designated as a person's medical and life "decision-maker," in the event of any such diminishment or loss of capacity. However, this is easier said than done. Choosing a caretaker and trusting that person to be a guardian and to make appropriate compassionate choices can be very challenging.

The relationships that were formed and revered during an elder person's lifetime take on new significance at this time. "Who can be trusted to act, speak and care for me when I am not able to do so?" is the million-dollar question for many elderly people. Sometimes, an attorney or physician is designated to coordinate the health and care of the person. The objectivity of a professional is preferred to the complexity of relationships with family members or relatives. In other instances, more than one person handles caretaking. Elderly couples may decide to involve all of their children in that capacity; significant decisions would then require a majority's rule.

The final preparations for and coordination of care, illness and death are fraught with emotion and psychological discomfort. Often, family therapy may be appropriate at this juncture. Offspring may resist and resent the role of caretaker. Unresolved issues with their parents and/or allegiances to their own families can result in conflict, guilt, anxiety, and anger. Sibling rivalry and family power dynamics can resurface when the aging parent situation requires cooperation and decision-making.

Usually, with an elderly couple, one partner dies before the other. There are several possible scenarios for the widow or widower's remaining life. If the deceased partner was ill for a long period and needed vigilant care, or if he or she suffered from any form of dementia, the partner likely has been the primary caretaker. The couple's relationship to each other and their attitudes toward the approaching loss and death impact the dynamic of their final months and years together. If the couple had a close and caring relationship, then the stressors of aging are generally better managed. If fears of loss and death were prevalent, then anxiety and poor management tends to dominate.

The release experienced from the loss of a partner is devastating, in either case. There is a constant awareness that you will be next. Again, attitude and inner resolves determine how the person left behind will handle and live out the rest of their time. Some people get very depressed and die within a year of their partner's death. Others embark on a frenzy of activity to complete as many experiences as they can in the time that remains for them. The partner left behind may even remarry.

Diets and food restrictions imposed by health problems are sometimes tossed out of the window. The lust to eat and taste and enjoy increases considerably. How people cope with dying is usually very similar to the ways they have coped with other issues faced throughout their life.

The following three short vignettes describe different experiences of issues that commonly present themselves during the end stage of life.

ೞೞೞ

Case Study: Mark and Agnes

Mark and Agnes had been married for fifty-seven years. He was eighty-five and she was seventy-seven years old. They had three children, two daughters and a son. They also had five grandchildren and three great-grandchildren.

Mark was very ill. He had severe cardio-vascular disease and Parkinson's. His condition was progressing rapidly toward further complications, and he was primarily bedridden. Agnes was relatively healthy. Other than lapses in memory and some incongruent behavior, she was doing fine and took care of Mark's needs. Their children were caring and offered help or funds, as they were able. When Mark was no longer able to eat and required surgery for a feeding tube, Jane, their eldest daughter, moved in with her parents to supervise and provide more vigilant care.

Jane had been divorced for a number of years but lived with a lover who was understanding and supportive of the situation, up to a point. She was a self-employed photographer with flexible hours and, therefore, the most likely candidate among her siblings to take on the caregiving.

However, the care of her parents became a fulltime job for Jane. She was hardly able to conduct her business, and her relationship with her lover collapsed. Mark died two years later. Agnes demonstrated more obvious signs of dementia. With limited finances, Jane became the sole party responsible for her mother. Agnes was sweet and affectionate but very hard to be around, as she repeated herself a thousand times and had no memory.

Jane's life became focused on her mother's care. She was angry with her siblings, since they had taken a back seat in this situation. She carried the full burden of responsibility. She felt both frustration and guilt for wanting her old life back. She believed that the role of caregiver had fallen on her shoulders by default rather than by choice, and she was resentful. Her issues seemed to be not with her mother so much as with her siblings.

Family therapy with all the siblings and any interested offspring would have been valuable in this case, in order to clarify the realities of the situation. This family had an ailing mother who was not in charge of her faculties and needed fulltime care. Agnes had made no provisions for her care in case of disability. Her children were her moral guardians. Jane could not have a life of her own *and* be her mother's sole caregiver.

How to proceed and distribute the demands of the care became the therapeutic question. Agnes's children had to confront their own willingness to be involved or not, and in what proportion. The work entailed achieving consensus and specific commitments to a course of action. The original relationships that each child had with their mother would guide and support the process and outcome. Any choice would have both positive and negative consequences, so these had to be explored. Each individual had to decide for themselves the extent of their ability and the time that they could contribute to their mother's care, along with what that would mean to them.

ଔଔଔଔ

Case Study: Bob and Harriet

Bob had been married to Harriet for twenty years. They had no children between them, but various children and grandchildren from previous marriages. Bob was seventy-three when Harriet was diagnosed with Alzheimer's at the age of sixty-five. Her disease progressed rapidly in severity, and she had to be institutionalized for proper care. She didn't recognize Bob, who visited her every day. She didn't recognize her children or any other family member. She mostly sat looking lost, smiling vacantly and either crying or singing softly to herself.

Bob sold their house and moved into an apartment close to the facility to be near at hand. Three years after being in assisted living, Harriet passed away. Bob was grief-stricken; however, he felt he had in essence lost his wife five years before. Despite his loss, Bob also experienced relief and liberation. He hid these feelings from the rest of his family and friends.

A year later, he moved again, into a nicer apartment in the heart of the city. He established a social life, dating online and visiting his grandchildren. He was looking for a third wife, as he wanted to share expenses and have a companion.

Individual therapy could clarify whether Bob's positive and forward-looking attitude had genuine depth or might be covering anxiety and fear regarding disease, death, and dying. He exhibited a frenzy of activity and a lust for life, which was admirable if somewhat off balance. It was appropriate for him to have some fear and anxiety about endings and death at this stage. Facing any fear is always a healthier approach than avoidance.

છ૨૯૩૯૨

Case Study: Maureen and John

Maureen and John had had five hip replacement surgeries between them. She was seventy-seven and he was eighty-four years old. They lived an active life, still playing tennis. In fact, most of their injuries were acquired while playing tennis. They also traveled, socialized, and enjoyed their grandchildren as much as possible. They took turns caring for each other when they were ill. They had a list of physicians and caregivers on hand and utilized them when necessary. They had made provisions for their deaths and in case of loss or disability. However, they did not regard themselves as old and resented being referred to as such. They believed that they had a long life ahead of them. Though somewhat slow, their minds were sharp and alert. They were involved in community life and participated in politics, casting their votes diligently. They were not interested in therapy, as they were confident about their coping skills.

The therapeutic concern here revolved around their strong unity and conjoint attitude toward their personal strengths and "long life" ahead. They had endured five hip replacement surgeries and yet continued to play tennis, regardless.

Their zest for life was remarkable and not to be tampered with. Yet there were traces of recklessness and denial in their behavior. Despite their frailness, they behaved like spring chickens and were in collusion with each other. A major concern was what would happen when one of them died? They were such a strong team together that the experience of the surviving partner could be traumatic.

Therapeutic intervention in this case presented philosophical quandaries. They were living the end of their lives fully and seemed to be enjoying themselves. They were present in the moment and yet ignored future possibilities and failed to take preventive measures. They were alert and in full mental faculty, plus they were not seeking help. They had made some key provisions in the event of grave illness and death, and made their lifestyle choices together. Maybe the best approach to this case was to let events unfold as they may and intervene only when the situation necessitated.

ଏଠାଠେ

CHILDREN

Working with children can be simpler and more rewarding in some respects than working with adults. At the same time, it can also be more challenging. The work is easier because a child's psychological defense mechanisms are not yet solidly built and access is more available. Children are less guarded and their psychological struggles are more on the surface. Having an impact on young minds from the early onset of problems can be most rewarding. While children are generally more amenable to change and learning new things, working with them can be a delicate undertaking. Children are undeveloped, dependent, and highly suggestible. Any therapeutic intervention has to be administered carefully so that guidance is not communicated as a command. A dominating force can overwhelm a child into obedience and adherence, changing the natural inclinations of the child's psyche.

The various growth patterns and needs in a child's developmental stages require different approaches to intervention and psychotherapy. Addressing each stage with knowledge, forethought and the appropriate tools will minimize the possible mishaps that a therapist could initiate.

The common denominator that makes working with children at all their stages of development different than working with adults is the therapist's ability to work outside of the box and their own comfort zones. The ability to be inventive and to change directions spontaneously in order to meet a child's needs is significant in the approaches utilized with children. Often the therapist may be required to sit on the floor, to be at the child's level and hold or comfort a crying child with touch. Sometimes therapists are compelled to leave the confines of their office and go to the playground in order to be more effective in communicating with a child. Physical and environmental flexibility is a useful technique for bonding with children.

Skillful use of art materials, drawings, pictures, film, music and songs, storytelling, and games are other modes of communication with children.

Children may not have the ability to vocalize their feelings nor have developed the cognitive means to express thoughts and describe what they understand. Observing the child closely in various staged activities is a key method for ascertaining the psychological dynamics and struggles that a child is experiencing.

When the child is non-verbal or is in a minimal-verbal stage of growth, the primary mode for assessment will be in behavior observation and through playing simple games.

Children at that stage of development will exhibit psychological disturbances through withdrawing behavior like sitting in a corner, not eating, not taking their normal naps, and/or non-participation in any of their normal routine activities. Their facial expressions will be congruent with the physical behavior and will express the feelings that cannot be verbalized. Excessive crying, outbursts of unusual anger, radical changes in normal sleep patterns, and regressions will also be the obvious indicators for disturbances.

When physical illnesses and discomfort are ruled out as possible causes, psychological intervention can take place. The initial steps involve interviewing everyone in the child's life in order to clarify key dynamics that are operating. Parents, siblings, the nanny, and pre-school personnel, and teachers are all significant members of a child's life. It is therefore appropriate to gather information about them and their interactions with the child in order to find clues about what might be causing a disturbance. In most cases, the main causes of problems are other people's behavior and the situations surrounding the child's life. However, there may be inherent conditions such as autism, learning disorders, and mental illnesses that are showing symptoms for the first time. Once an accurate diagnosis of the situation has been made, therapeutic remedies can then be put into motion.

At the age when a child has developed more cognition, play therapy, drawings, and storytelling can be used to gather indirect data that may reveal psychological disturbances. The storytelling technique is the most useful way to understand a child's learned coping skills. This technique is tailored to depict the dynamics of what the therapist deduces to be the current struggles in a child's life. The therapist creates and begins a story that resembles the child's condition. The child picks up the story and continues it to the end, if possible. A lot of information can be revealed for the therapist's assessment with this technique. The child's struggles and coping skills will become apparent through his or her own account of the problems encountered in the story. The therapist can offer alternate coping and problem solving methods for the story's characters to try in order to get them out of difficult situations. This is an indirect modeling and teaching device that helps a child develop better coping skills.

Sand play and playing with dolls and household models are another way for a child to describe what is occurring in his or her life. More verbal communication comes into play as the child grows; they become able to express their needs and describe their dilemmas. It is important to use language that is at the child's level of comprehension and emotional maturity. Children vary in their rate of development from one to another. The therapist has to individualize his or her approach in order to bond and connect with a child of any age and developmental stage.

Preteens and teenagers are in an interim stage of development. They are neither adults nor children but contain growth levels that are both mature and childish. This age group requires an expert adult for guidance but not an authority figure who imposes incomprehensible rules and regulations on their behavior. An authentic, forthright, caring therapist can usually have an impact on members of this age group.

Teenagers are quite capable of having insights and seeing beyond face values. They usually separate themselves from adults and have their own subculture. Preteens have a tendency to idolize their teenage mentors and teenage siblings. Friendships and specific group bonding impose strict social structures on their worlds. Their allegiances to specific groups are indicative of their separation process from parental and adult authorities. They are in the developmental phase of individuating and becoming their own person. This is a rough period for most teenagers. It is difficult to select and choose values, and define yourself outside of the parental realms. It is also a rough period for parents, as they experience the diminishment of their authority and loss of impact on their children.

Teenagers experience volatile hormonal changes in their bodies that motivate mood swings and impulsive behavior. Usually they take themselves and their feelings very seriously. They may act out on these feelings without much forethought; this can lead to their encountering dangerous and risky situations. Experimentation is important for learning and growth. However, an understanding of the impact of the natural biological changes in the body can give a teenager some perspective on their feelings of turmoil and provide them with some coping skills.

The therapist has an opportunity to become the adult person in whom the teenager can confide as they develop a stronger sense of self and explore life's issues and relationships. Confidentiality is paramount for winning the trust of a teenager. With younger children, legal parameters dictate the inclusion of parents in the therapeutic process. With teenagers, even though they are below the legal age and still considered minors, confidential boundaries have to be understood, respected, and agreed to by the parents. Having privacy from parents is perhaps the major change in a teenager's desires. This struggle is a significant step toward individuation. The need for privacy is usually difficult for parents to accept. Some family sessions in the presence of the teen are often useful. The purpose of the sessions is to agree to ground rules and to enlarge the parameters of freedom as the child grows into adulthood.

ଓଓଓଓ

Case Study: Sally

The following case study is an example of a therapeutic encounter with a child.

Sally is eight years old but looks much younger. She was brought in for therapy due to her school's strong insistence. Her mother, Donna, did not appear to be too concerned. She believed that Sally was going through a "phase" and was just being "moody." Sally did not say much. She was quiet, played with her fingers, and looked around without much interest.

The school's reports indicated that Sally did well in her classes but behaved in strange, inappropriate ways. The inappropriate behaviors were described as laughter when something serious or solemn was being discussed and tears when something humorous or funny came up in her classes. These incongruent responses left her teachers and classmates amazed and caused disruptions. Sally was also not reachable. She seemed to be in a constant daydream state. Again, this behavior was not congruent with her grades. She had to be listening, since she did well on tests and excelled both in math and English composition. Her spelling was somewhat off but not below average. The school had deduced that some emotional and/or mental issues had to be causing Sally's strange behavior and insisted on psychotherapeutic intervention.

Sally lived primarily with her mother, Donna, who worked as a set designer in film. Her father was a physicist and college professor. He and Donna had divorced when Sally was five. In the past year, the father had remarried a woman whom Sally liked, but her father's new wife had two other girls from a previous marriage. Sally's stepsisters were twelve and nine years old. She visited her father on occasion and shared a room with Mary, the nine-year-old. It became apparent that Sally did not like her stepsisters and held a sullen anger toward her father.

Sally's mom, Donna, was a party girl. She had a full social life and attended late night events for work. Sally often accompanied her mother to these night events and wound up falling asleep on some couch before her mother took her home. Even though Sally spent a good deal of time with her mother and felt loved by her, she wasn't sure if her mother could truly see her and be available for her. Her father was remote and more interested in his new family.

Sally loved to draw and her skills at drawing were remarkable, so art and drawing became a way in to therapy with Sally. She was asked to make three drawings: 1) the living room where her parents lived before the divorce; 2) the current living room at her father's house; and 3) the living room with her mother. She was asked to imagine an everyday event and to place each of the household's residents in their designated places in the living rooms.

The first drawing before the divorce showed Sally as a little girl sitting on a couch in front of a TV. Mom and Dad were in the dining area in close combat position with gaping mouths, shouting at each other. The second drawing showed her father and stepmom cuddled on the couch. Her stepsisters sat around the dining table playing a game while Sally stood separate in a corner, watching the family. In the third drawing, Sally sat behind a computer. Her mother and several friends were gathered around the coffee table in conversation with drinks in their hands.

In all three drawings, Sally was separate from the others and their activities. She was by herself, alone and isolated. The depictions of isolation were consistent with the other information that had been gathered. Both parents were shown to be more involved in their own lives than hers, and Sally seemed to be on the periphery.

Sally was quite capable of being articulate but was reticent to offer or initiate conversations. The storytelling technique was utilized here also, in order to stimulate more revelations. The therapist began a story that Sally continued, taking it to a place where the conflicts clearly reflected her current psychological state.

⟅⟆⟅⟆

The Story Telling Technique

The therapist began the story:

Once upon a time, there was a little princess who was very bright and pretty. She loved to read, to draw, and to play in the garden. Her mother, the queen, was fun-loving and gave grand parties, inviting all the important people of the nearby kingdoms to dance, sing, and have lots of fun. Her father, the king, was always very busy, traveling around his kingdom and taking care of his subjects. He was hardly ever home at the castle. When he came home, he always brought a present for the princess but nothing for the queen. The king and queen didn't seem to like each other.

One day, the king left to roam about his kingdom but forgot to say goodbye to the princess. Some days later, a letter arrived to say he was going to live in a new castle and have a new family, but the princess was invited to visit him whenever she wanted.

Sally picked up the story:

The princess was very sad. She was also angry with her mother the queen for letting her father move away from them.

Secretly, she put some clothes in a bag and decided to run away and search for her father's new castle. She wanted to stop him before he found a new family and wanted to bring him home. She had to cross the forest. She walked a long time and was afraid of the animals.

Finally, as it was getting dark and really scary, she was able to see the castle. But the castle was surrounded by water. There was no bridge or boat for her to cross. She didn't want to swim in the ugly dark water. She was forced to spend the night in a tree. She was very uncomfortable, cold, and scared.

In the morning a bridge came down and she ran across to reach the castle's door. She knocked at the door for a long time. No one came to let her in. When an old woman opened the door carrying a basket, the princess was able to slip by her and get in. She ran up the stairs looking for her father.

In a big room, she saw her father with a new queen and two little girls. They looked very happy and were eating their breakfast. They didn't notice her. She was tired, hungry, dirty, and very cold. When she called out to her father, he didn't seem to hear or see her. No one saw her. She discovered that she had become invisible. She couldn't see her hands or any part of her body either. Something must have happened while she was sleeping in the tree. Something magical had turned her into nothingness.

The therapist continued the story to create an outcome that involved rescue and recovery:

Meanwhile, at the castle home, the mother queen was frantic with worry. She couldn't find her little princess daughter, and she had looked everywhere. The queen summoned her soldiers, and they rode into the forest to search the outer limits. They found no trace. Finally, the queen decided to ride to the king's other castle and ask for his help.

She reached the other castle at breakneck speed and told the king about their daughter's disappearance. The little princess heard everything. She was sitting, huddled in a big chair by the fireplace, but no one could see her. She kept crying out, "Mother, Father, I am here." No one could hear her, either.

The queen paced about, very agitated. She could not imagine where else to look. The king asked her to calm down and sit by the fire. He gave her a cup of milk to drink. Unknown to everyone, the chair the queen sat on was the same chair where the princess was sitting.

The queen was uncomfortable sitting in this chair and felt lumps on the cushions. She got up to see what was bothering her and accidentally tipped the cup of milk. It drenched the princess, and lo and behold, the princess became visible. The mother queen was ecstatic with joy and wonder. She fell on her knees to hug her daughter and showered her with kisses. The king also cried in delight and joined them. All three held one another, crying, kissing, embracing, and laughing. The little princess felt warm and loved at last.

Her parents told the princess over and over how much they loved her and how special she was to them. No one could possibly replace her, no matter what happened. She belonged to them forever and ever.

The princess asked her father to come back home to their castle. But the king said that wherever he was, and in whichever castle he lived, her place was always in his heart forever and nothing could take that away. The queen agreed and also reassured the princess that she was always going to belong to them and they belonged to her. Absolutely nothing could ever change this truth.

Usually, as the story unfolds and progresses, the child grasps the similarities between the fairy tale and his or her own life. Contributions and embellishments to the story are encouraged. The twists and turns and outcomes can be retold and other options can be revised in order to suit the psychology of the child in question.

ରେ ରେ ରେ

Psychological Dynamics

Clearly, Sally's acting out behaviors in school raised the alarm about the depression and isolation that she had been feeling. She felt invisible to both her parents; school was the place where she could express her cry for help.

In the drawings and the storytelling exercise, Sally was able to describe very poignantly her feelings of abandonment and becoming invisible. She had been secretly devastated when her parents divorced. She experienced further heartache when her father remarried. She believed that her father had replaced her with the new stepsisters. She didn't think she belonged to him as his daughter. She thought that he now belonged to his new family and that she had no right to him.

Sally's relationship with her mother was a constant but was taken for granted. Donna took Sally around like a piece of luggage rather than as a person with individual needs and a will of her own.

Family therapy was highly recommended. It appeared that the parents had failed to actually explain their divorce to their daughter. They had neglected to reassure Sally about her place in their separate lives. Ground rules, visitation rights, special times to spend with one another, and co-parenting strategies had never been discussed or implemented. As it was, Sally stayed with her mother and saw her father haphazardly, based on whims and requests. A consistent schedule had not been constructed in order to create a sense of security for the child.

Family therapy would attempt to clarify for the parents that the decisions they had made around their divorce, remarriage, and individual lives had great impact on their child. They appeared to have gone about their divorce and remarriage without considering Sally's need for reassurance and stability. Sally had been expected to cope and come to terms with whatever the parents had decided. No explanation or crisis management had been offered.

When the parents divorced, they had understood that Donna would have full custody of Sally, yet no legal documents had been signed. The father's responsibilities and involvement in Sally's life remained vague. He occasionally contributed funds and paid some outstanding bills. Even though the mother had assumed full custody informally, she had not proven herself fully capable of being available as required of such a responsibility. Donna's work and lifestyle always took priority over Sally's needs. Family therapy helped the divorced parents realize that devising a co-parenting arrangement would benefit all three participants and enhance Sally's wellbeing.

Sally felt very uncomfortable with her father's new family. She felt that her position with her father had been usurped. A co-parenting plan needed to invite the father's new wife to participate. Appropriate boundaries and time schedules between the two families needed to be established in order to ensure smooth transitions.

An exploration of the potential relationships between the stepsisters would be taken more slowly. Only time and experience would show whether or not a friendship was likely. First, however, ground rules and cooperative structures needed to be implemented in order to ease the entries of the children in and out of one another's lives. Similar interests and activities could be explored as a bridge for the three stepsisters to come together. All of the girls needed some time to get to know one another so that they could build trust and find openings for bonding.

Sally needed to experience firsthand that her father's devotion toward his own daughter was on firm ground and not in jeopardy because he had daughters who were now dividing his attention. He needed to prove through action and behavior, not just words, that his connection to Sally was solid no matter what happened, and that it would not dissolve like his marriage had to her mother.

Sally had very little trust or sense of security with either parent. These were the wounds that had initiated her cries for help. Therefore, the first orders of business in the therapeutic process were to win her trust and establish safety through explicit, tangible ground rules adhered to by all parties involved.

ପ୍ରପ୍ରପ୍ର

SINGLEHOOD

Much has been written regarding discrimination and prejudice against race, ethnicities, classes, and religions. Not much is available, however, on the prejudices in all societies around the globe toward people who are single and who do not live their lives with a family or a mate. In today's world, the state of singlehood is growing rapidly. Yet the privilege and status enjoyed by people who are couples and/or have families are regularly denied to those people who live their lives in singlehood.

Shame and failure are often attributed to people who are single. Even those who have consciously chosen to embark on being alone have internalized some aspects of this shame and failure that is projected by the culture. Others view not having found a mate as "abnormal" behavior. The common opinion of people in most cultures is that there must be something wrong with any person who has failed to have a family and who lives alone. Some examples of such beliefs are:

- ❖ This person must not know how to compromise
- ❖ This person is too selfish
- ❖ This person must have hidden secrets
- ❖ This person is afraid of commitments

- ❖ This person is afraid to experience the joys of parenthood
- ❖ This person is too ugly to be selected

Choosing a single lifestyle consciously is not acceptable behavior in most societies.

From an economic perspective, living as a single person incurs higher costs. Nothing in society is structured to be financially advantageous for the single person. Couples and families enjoy discounts; sales are tailored for their needs. Communities rarely provide any sort of benefit for singles.

Attending social functions can be embarrassing and anxiety-provoking for someone single, especially for single women. In social gatherings, having an escort is expected and understood as "normal"; attending a function alone is considered odd and peculiar. The lone female is either barely tolerated and discounted or is considered fair game to be encroached upon.

Men who do not have permanent relationships are labeled as "playboys" or thought to have peculiarities that cause them to be rejected by potential mates. Women who remain alone are labeled as "too smart for their own good," "too undesirable," and/or "not natural in their sexual proclivities."

Mothers worry when their children pass an age and are still living a single life. Young women seem to be in a frenzy to find mates, projecting a fear of being left alone and left behind. Men start to think about having families only when their buddies start to win the procreation race by having children. To remain alone is to be a misfit or a loser, someone regarded with pity by his or her community.

In psychotherapy, single people express both self-doubt and confusion about the cultural condemnation imposed on them. Their choice to live alone is under speculation. They are concerned that something must indeed be wrong since they are not behaving according to the natural expectations of their family and community.

They also see themselves as misfits and worry that somehow, by being single, they got the short end of the stick and have lost their chance to experience happiness in the ways that are considered "normal." By feeling different and separate from their culture's expected norms, single people can internalize the projected prejudices. They may experience turmoil, depression, identity crises, and anxiety.

In light of choosing to be alone and without a life partner, single people develop and adopt behavior that supports this lifestyle. They learn to be self-reliant, self-contained, and independent individuals. They are also self-motivated and non-reactive as they pursue and attain their goals. These characteristics and behavior choices, as in all choices, have advantages and disadvantages. It is productive and healthy to be self-motivated and independent. But it is also difficult for another person to penetrate and find room in this lifestyle. This lifestyle has been designed to support and perpetuate a solo existence.

Asking for company and help are usually conducted within parameters that do not invite further intimacies. Yet the main complaint that the single person expresses in therapy is an existential feeling of aloneness. They often believe that "aloneness" is subjected only to people who live solo. It is difficult for a single person to imagine that people who are in committed and long-term relationships *also* experience existential "aloneness," on occasion.

As the single person ages, the inevitable needs for aid and care by others arise. For them, it is very difficult to relax their reins of autonomy and self-reliance. The solo individual has lived a lifetime with the dictum of being alone and independent. Yet the realities of aging demand certain dependence and often necessitate care by other people. This disconcerting reality forces the solo person to accept and come to terms with the limitations of life and everyone's inevitable aging.

A regret often expressed by single people is about their being childless. They have feelings of remorse and loss connected to the notion of ending their inherited genetic line, and not passing it on to the next generation. Death feels more final and the end, more concrete. Not having offspring can also mean dying alone, without anyone significant to mourn their loss. In the case of ill health during old age, there are no trusted offspring to administer care and to be present.

There are no guaranteed outcomes in any choices made in life. As in all cases, flexibility and adaptability to all stages of life's process are essential for constructive survival.

ରାରାରା

Case Study: Sophia

The following case study profiles Sophia, a woman living a solo lifestyle.

Everyone in Sophia's family imagined that she would marry early and have a dozen kids. No one believed that she had any other interests regarding her future. Sophia daydreamed of hot romance and a special prince who would kiss her awake and carry her off into the sunset. However, she also daydreamed about becoming a doctor and joining world organizations that would allow her to do good in third world countries. The aspiration to be a doctor became her primary goal. Finding a mate and becoming a mother were wishes that she looked forward to, but were never her main ambitions in life.

With hard work and due diligence she achieved her primary goal and joined Doctors Without Borders (MSF). She traveled extensively in Africa and other remote parts of the world, and was finally stationed in Guatemala. At that juncture, she was single, forty-five years old, and leading a fulfilling life. She had had a few relationships that might have grown into something deeper, but in the final analysis her work always took precedence and competed for her time and attention. Sophia was resigned to being single. She didn't believe that she would ever find a life partner who would allow her commitment to her work to come first in life.

Her family never understood or approved of her choices. They did not consider her to be a "normal" woman with "normal" inclinations. She had three other sisters and a brother who had all married and had a score of children. Sophia was the baby of the family and a favorite aunt for her nieces and nephews. Her siblings were not reconciled to her singlehood and were constantly matchmaking when she visited home. They were relentless in their efforts to lure her away from the lifestyle that she had carved for herself. Choosing work over procreation and family was not in her family's repertoire.

Sophia appeared very capable, articulate, professional, and dedicated to her world of medicine. On a personal level, she was unequipped and somewhat at a loss as to how to conduct herself. She was attractive with a trim, athletic body, but was unaware of her impact and beauty.

At the age fifty she came home to live near her family and set up a medical practice. She volunteered part time at the local free clinic. As a physician she automatically had the respect of the community. However, there was much gossip and curiosity about her being alone, a fifty-year-old woman who had never married and who had traveled around the world by herself.

For Sophia, coming home also signified a readiness to finally consider looking for a mate and life partner. At the age of fifty, however, she was firmly habituated to living her life according to her own needs and planned agendas. She was thoroughly independent and a clear authority figure. To the delight and encouragement of her family, she was introduced to numerous men as possible candidates. Unfortunately these men were either intimidated by her strong presence and high achievements or were looking to be mothered and taken care of. Soon, Sophia withdrew from the dating pool in frustration and resolved once again to live her life solo. But she felt very lonely and worried about aging alone. She decided to seek psychotherapy.

ೞೞೞೞ

Psychological Dynamics

At the age of fifty, Sophia was an attractive, healthy, accomplished woman with a lot to offer any partner in a relationship. She was lonely and hoped ideally to find a mate; still, it was not clear whether she was willing to adapt and adjust her behavior in order to be open to living with the idiosyncrasies of another person. She was so good at living alone and accustomed to deciding life's course and direction with only her own needs to consider.

It was likely that most men she encountered in her age group would be divorced with previous marriages and offspring. Whether she would be willing to include the "baggage" of these potential life partners as candidates had yet to be discovered. In fact, it was prudent for her to draw up a list of advantages for being in a relationship versus disadvantages, just as a reality check.

Sophia was not used to settling for less than what she wanted. Clarifying her willingness to be flexible and adaptable in forming a permanent relationship was the first step in the therapeutic process. Provided that Sophia agreed to change the dynamics of her solo existence, she could then explore the possibilities of what another person's participation might add to her life.

The second step for therapy was to help Sophia become more self-aware of the outward persona that she projected. Although she was attractive, warm, and had appealing manners, she also conveyed her strong self-containment, as though she did not need any another person. This projection would not invite a man to approach her. In fact, it was a sign that communicated for her to be left alone. This was incongruent with her goal. Therapy helped her to develop gestures that would signal her welcoming overtures of interest.

Sophia was unaware of her beauty and handled her social life as though she were in professional consultations. She kept her privacy closely guarded and did not communicate on personal levels. She had never considered her impact as a woman. She found that she was more attracted and receptive to men who were much younger than she. Unfortunately, these young men did not reciprocate the attraction. Helping Sophia discover this self-awareness allowed her to participate more fully in the courtship dances that occur between men and women on their path to making final partnership selections.

Singlehood

If Sophia was indeed ready to be fully involved in building a relationship, she needed to explore some factors that women face developmentally at a much younger age. In her individual process, she had skipped that stage of development most women experience in their twenties when looking for a mate. In her twenties, Sophia was in the throes of medical school and preparing to embark for Africa. At fifty, she was clueless about most social interactions between men and women.

Sophia's body was also no longer young and vibrant. She was in middle age and could not compete with the twenty-year-old women. She experienced self-doubts and had some body image issues. She had nostalgia for the body she used to have when she was twenty and could hold her own. Coming to terms with what was past and with the choices she made when she was at the peak of her female power and sexuality warranted close attention and understanding. Sophia's self-exploration and developing self-awareness helped her choose whether she was willing to give up her solo lifestyle and participate in the mating rituals and dances required, in order to find a relationship.

It was unclear whether Sophia's mentioned loneliness was an existential angst or a fear of aging alone. It needed to be clarified for her that experiencing existential aloneness was not restricted to people who lived alone without family or mate. Existential loneliness is a human condition felt by everyone. People in all walks of life, in the most intimate moments even, can experience a disconnection and feel alone. Families, life partners, religion, and a busy social life cannot alleviate the feelings of ultimate aloneness ever-present in the human condition. If Sophia could look objectively at her siblings with their many offspring, she would note that they, too, felt lonely and alone at times, even in the midst of their large families.

Sophia expressed some concern and fear regarding her aging alone without a network set up to assist her, in case of illness. She needed reassurance that she should explore various options and methods of securing help for the various needs she might encounter as she aged. Developing insurances for the aging process would be a good idea, regardless of her success in finding a mate.

Sophia's primary objective was to choose whether she would still be happier living solo or, now that she was available, prefer to be committed to a permanent relationship. Whatever choice one made, the opposite of that choice would always be attractive. As previously indicated, there are advantages and disadvantages to any choice made. The weight of the appropriate choice is measured on the grand scale of its pros and cons. Reconciling and coming to terms with any final decision that is implemented is the objective of therapy. Choosing a solo lifestyle can be a viable and positive way of life for some people. Sophia had to consider her personality, her needs, and her options in order to make a decision that would enhance her present life.

ଚ୍ଚଚ୍ଚ

MULTICULTURAL & MULTIRACIAL IDENTITIES

When a person is the product of more than one culture, ethnicity and/or race, the potential to see and experience the world differently opens to them. These differences in having multiple origins stand in marked contrast to people who grow up solely within one culture, ethnicity, or race. The potential and opportunities for these differences to emerge and be adopted depend on an individual's personal struggles, goals, desires, and psychological reactions to being from a mixture of origins.

The multicultural and/or multiracial person has the potential to cross boundaries and to adopt and choose the favored characteristics from their inherited cultures. The potential to cross boundaries isn't limited only to one's inherited cultures; learning can be expanded and utilized to include a leap to other cultures, as well. The unicultural person identifies with the characteristics of the single culture to which he or she has been exposed and operates primarily within its boundaries. The ability to leap across cultural boundaries is what defines the multicultural person. However, not belonging to one particular root system has its own trials and tribulations. An individual's psychology and process of maturation will determine the positive and negative consequences of having multicultural origins.

The identities and roles developed in a person are usually in accordance with or in reaction to cultural expectations. Societies that are patriarchal or matriarchal dictate gender roles, behavior, and sexual attitudes for their members. An individual's psychological reactions to any of the dictates imposed by their culture play a major part in these configurations. There can be adherence to or rebellion against the rules and standards outlined for behavior. There are cultures that are that religiously based and others that are reactions to religious rules. Education and class and the distributions of wealth also define the cultural interactions between people.

There are marked differences between urban and rural lifestyles. Natural environments and settings set parameters for the expression of culture in people's lives. Beach communities have their own unique casualness in clothes and behavior. City life inspires an entirely different wardrobe, set of activities, and pace in the fast lane. Small communities bring people closer, while large cities separate and disconnect people from one another. A person who is a bi-product of more than one set of cultural expectations can usually cross boundaries and, when exposed to unknown situations, adapt more easily to changes and differences.

The mindset of multicultural individuals may or may not be amenable to accepting the mixture of their origins. The choices are open, but these people are dependent on the psychological consequence of their life experiences and maturation processes. A multicultural person appears to experience certain developmental stages that form his or her mixed identity. The struggle to discover a identity and to develop a self-concept usually occurs during the time when a child is exposed to socialization.

The first stage of development for a multicultural and/or multiracial person is usually marked by a state of confusion. The recognition of being different and apart from "the mainstream" is encountered at this stage. Not having points of reference, not belonging to any one obvious group, feeling apart and undefined are all some of the initial reactions and experiences of a multicultural person.

The realization that the choice to decide who you are and where you belong is the responsibility of the individual is an aspect of the second stage of development. Having this choice is both disturbing and liberating. Multicultural people mostly choose to connect with and embrace the "mainstream" aspects of themself during this second stage. The need to belong, to connect with the norms, and to not feel alienated is of paramount importance during this developmental stage.

For example: a bi-racial child is comforted by the decision to embrace the parts of themselves that are white and reinforced by the culture as superior and better. This period can be disillusioning for the growth process of the individual. The emphasis on one part in someone's make-up and the denial of other parts also occurs. The person who is of mixed origins is in essence relating to and communicating with only certain parts of themselves. They are negating, even rejecting, other aspects of their origin under the illusion of wanting to belong. Inevitably, the choices of this stage will not be constructive for the mental health and wellbeing of the individual. Choosing only those parts of oneself that identify with the "mainstream" will eventually collapse. Also, the "mainstream" culture not only does not approve of or embrace people of mixed origins, but often rejects them. Encountering this reality provokes an alienating realization for the multicultural person.

During the third stage of development (which usually occurs in the late teen years and in young adults), the pendulum shifts and an individual tends to celebrate and connect with aspects of their origins that are ethnic and opposed to "mainstream" expectations. This stage defines and brings forth parts of the identity that have been slumbering and pushed to the back of the psyche. There is a growth spurt and positive flow experienced during this stage. The multicultural person believes that, by connecting to their ethnic origins, they are connecting to their roots, and can finally belong to a group or groups that can serve as their foundation, support, and be a source for inspiration. Unfortunately, even though there are many positive aspects to this choice, the denial of the other parts in a whole person's gestalt also damages the full expression and possibility of a multicultural identity. The communities that host people of ethnic origins do not welcome or allow inclusion of people of mixed origins in their circles. Once again, the person of mixed origins is confronted with not having an identity that belongs to any one specific group and faces the responsibility of constructing his or her identity.

The fourth stage is the healing stage, whereby the multicultural person realizes that they are a mixture of cultures, races, and ethnicities. All parts have validity and are sources for knowledge, expansion, and richness. Denying any part of an individual's psyche and make-up is ultimately harmful and closes off the blossoming of the full self. There is a feeling of peace and calm in this stage of development. The acceptance of all parts is healing and opens up the possibility to consider and appreciate the advantages connected with being a mixture.

The transitions through these four stages of development sometimes do not occur smoothly. The multicultural person can get stuck in one stage or another, and resist the natural progression into and discovery of the next phase. The timing for each stage of development is also very personal. An individual's denial system may be too overpowering in the face of wanting to belong. Society's prejudices, dogmas, and discriminations may hinder the person's growth or discourage them from embracing all aspects of their multicultural origins. The individual can remain in denial and reject those parts of their heritage that are not condoned by the society within which they live.

If the person is able to withstand the pressures and allow the progression toward forming a positive identity, then there are undeniable advantages to being multicultural and to learning how to wear several hats without experiencing conflicts.

As discussed previously, the primary advantage of the multicultural person is that their identity formations are not restricted to one set of standards imposed by the expectations of one culture. Multicultural people are unique in that they can select and choose from the various cultures, aspects, and characteristics that suit their needs and personality. This freedom of choice enables the psyche to be more open, conscious and accepting of differences among people of all walks of life.

When they travel, they can feel a sense of belonging to the world rather than just to one group of people. The possibilities to connect and understand other cultures are a learning opportunity that a multicultural person has already undertaken as they come to understand and accept their own multicultural origins. Differences among others are not as disconcerting or difficult to grasp and accept. The bridge that connects differences is already built into a multicultural person's origins and constitution.

The disadvantages of a multicultural identity are felt mostly in the conscious and unconscious views expressed by others. It is still common in society to exclude, ostracize, and alienate people who are mixtures and who do not specifically belong to a set group. People are often uncomfortable when they cannot explain someone's race or ethnicity in simplistic terms.

Not belonging to any specific group can be experienced as lonely. It is even difficult to belong to a group of people who are all multicultural. Each person of mixed origins has had unique experiences in choosing and defining their identity. Hardly any two multicultural people with similar backgrounds can be viewed as the same. The experiences and selection processes are so unique and individual that grouping multicultural people into a category for the purposes of definition is difficult to accomplish.

Current trends forecast that societies and cultures in the near future will be comprised of many people with multicultural and multiracial origins. The consequences of such a complex new world remain to be experienced.

ಇ3ಇ3ಇ3

Case Study: **Reza**

The following case study describes the struggles of a multicultural person.

Reza was the only child of Egyptian parents. He was born in the U.S. and considered himself to be fully American. However, his heritage had been kept alive by his parents, and he spoke Arabic fluently.

He came for psychotherapy when he was in his third year at UCLA. He needed to make some decisions regarding his future so that he could plan accordingly. Reza's appearance was interesting and spoke volumes. At first glance he looked, walked, and carried himself like an African-American rapper or Ali-G incarnate. He was tall and slender with his jeans falling short of his hips exposing eight inches of royal blue underwear. The bottoms of his trouser legs dragged on the floor. He wore gleaming white, high-tech sneakers with their Velcro straps undone. His head was shaved close to one side of his skull while long dreadlock strands hung from the other. His gait had a sideways swing and, as he walked, long gold chains hung out of his pockets, swaying in rhythm with his body.

He began by stating immediately that he had been inspired to seek therapy by watching Tony Soprano and his psychiatrist on the HBO program *The Sopranos*.

Regardless of his affectations and defenses, Reza was an extremely bright and ambitious student. He was considering graduate school for a Ph.D. either in political science or literature. He was also interested in law school. Sometimes, he thought that his best option was to stick to his music and promote his rap band. He was not sure which path to follow. He had started to feel anxious, which had led to some erectile difficulties.

Reza stated that he was in a quandary. He believed that he could be many things and do them well, but could not decide what was best for him. He had applied to well-known schools for law, political science and literature, and had received some acceptances. The choices all felt interesting to him but not quite the "right" path to commit to. His parents held anti-establishment views and could not understand his interest in pursuing a law degree. He was drawn to scholarly endeavors both in literature and political science; but believed that following those avenues could lead only to professorships. Becoming a professor felt old and unadventurous at this point in his life.

Reza loved his music and playing in his band but only considered it half-seriously as a full-time profession. He was unable to see himself only as a rapper.

He had an Iranian-American girlfriend; she hung out with the "beaners," Iranian-Americans who behaved like and emulated Mexican-Americans. He and his girlfriend's primary activity was to salsa dance.

The members of Reza's band were all multicultural people. He was the rap artist. The drummer was born in India. There were two Brazilian girls on the guitar and a Norwegian fellow on keyboard.

When exploring his family's background and heritage, Reza did not show much interest in, or affiliation with, Egypt or his Egyptian origins. He described himself as a "man on the street," even though his parents were both physicians and he had been brought up in an upper middle class neighborhood. The incongruities with his demeanor, his ambitions, his origins and the presenting persona were numerous. Clearly Reza had been crossing cultural boundaries both within himself and through his relationships with friends without any special or specific direction. It seemed as though he was trying on different garments and experimenting with a variety of styles and roles. A specific fit and identity had not emerged.

He seemed to be in the middle of a search and, perhaps, had become a little lost and without a compass.

ରୁରୁରୁ

Psychological Dynamics

Looking at Reza from the perspective of his connections to the heart, mind, and genitals, it appeared that his connections between the mind and genitals were potent while the connection to his heart was missing. He had strong ambitions plus the drives to implement them. However, his passions seemed to be controlled by his mind rather than by his heart. He had not experienced nor felt his choices for the future from his heart. He had given himself the option to explore without feeling the pull to commit to one direction. All of the options sounded viable and good to him, but he didn't know and couldn't *feel* the passion for what he wanted most.

The rejection of his heritage was a red flag in the sense that he had been denying a deep part of himself from entering his consciousness. Instead, he had chosen a black rap-star identity as his outer persona to present to the world. His parents were Egyptian, yet none of his friends or band members reinforced that heritage. When questioned about his origins, Reza was dismissive. He declared that any association with the Middle East was like being a pariah. He emphasized that he was American-born and had never been to Egypt; it was not a part of him. His parents were not completely American, but *he* was.

From these statements, one could deduce that maybe Reza rejected his origins because he viewed the society at large as having a negative reaction toward anything Egyptian. He wanted approval and wanted to belong. He couldn't fit in with the "white majority," so he adopted an image that was supposedly "cool," apart from the mainstream but certainly admired and accepted in its own sector. He was a rap artist or wanted to emulate the look of one.

When his appearance was commented upon, Reza lit up. He explained that his band was called "Split," and he was trying to project the "Split" with his hair arrangement. Seemingly, the title of "Split" had much deeper connotations than purely cosmetic representation. It could not just be taken at face value.

The focus of psychotherapeutic intervention was for him to grasp the notions of "Split," and to expand on its meanings, ramifications, and impact on his personality development. This mode for entry easily captured his attention and participation. Reza's identity had been scattered loosely between boundaries of various cultures. It was an extreme reaction to being multicultural, like walking through an international maze filled with hidden clues but with Reza remaining elusive.

He had constructed and experimented with images in his mind and had a good deal of youthful energy and even daring. His heart or vulnerabilities, however, were shut down and out of reach. The anxieties and erectile dysfunction that he had been experiencing were marked clues: openings to explore his other dimensions and any wounds that he may have sustained in the formation of his self-concept. He had specific blocks that needed careful tending; they were strong indicators of those hidden wounds.

Making peace with his heritage and including it in his persona and consciousness were not easily attainable. There were many resistances to overcome, and each resistance offered further insight into the dynamic process that indicated the direction of his psychotherapy. Eventually these obstacles had to be overcome in order for his healing and full self-acceptance to take place.

Helping Reza to connect, embrace, and include his heritage in his conscious awareness and behaviors moved him to the third developmental stage of his multicultural identity. When the pendulum swung to the other side of the equation, the rejection of "mainstream" roles and values and the glorification of his ethnic origins could occur.

People who have extreme natures may become radicalized at this junction. Given Reza's age and youthful fervor, an extreme reaction could have been possible. Conscious awareness of one's developmental stages can sometimes help a person understand the character of each stage and what it demands. The patience to experience and follow through with what is learned and gained from each stage of development has therapeutic power. The transition into the fourth stage of development is the ultimate goal of psychotherapy; at this place, healing and cohesion can fall into place.

Multicultural & Multiracial Identities

It is already a given that a multicultural person wears several hats, according to their background. Acquiring the ability to switch hats smoothly and without disturbance from inner and outer conflict is an art that can be learned and adopted. Even though the need to switch hats seems obvious to the objective eye, it comes as a revelation to most multicultural people.

Normally, it does not occur to individuals of mixed origin that different hats are appropriate for different occasions. Most multicultural people tend to wear all of their hats simultaneously; that is the multicultural person's comfortable, natural way of being. At other times, conflicts and miscommunication are experienced when presenting various aspects of their many facets at inopportune moments.

Switching hats as the situation demands is an artful and tricky undertaking. In one sense, cohesion and inclusion are the healing answers for a person with multicultural splits in their origins. Yet the effective act of switching hats demands a compartmentalization of the different parts of one's heritage that are lodged in the personality. The challenge is learning how to compartmentalize so that one's communications are appropriate for the situation without losing sight of the larger picture of the self. The overseer in an individual's psyche always needs to be awake and alert in order to conduct the multi-cultural orchestra within.

With practice, switching hats can be accomplished easily. In fact, as the multicultural or multiracial person learns the art of switching hats, they develop an acute awareness of the boundaries and difference in cultural expressions. For the multi-origin person, it is easier to assume differences unconsciously rather than have conscious awareness. However, acquired awareness creates and shapes better skills for effective communication without experiencing extreme splits and divisions within the self.

While communicating various aspects of their multifaceted heritage, the multicultural or multiracial person remains in touch with his or her gestalt, and is able to maneuver smoothly between and within its boundaries.

ଜ୍ଞଜ୍ଞ

THE MALE/FEMALE SPECTRUM

The conviction that men and women are different seems to be lodged in the collective unconscious of all humans, and has been passed on since the beginning of time. Children are raised in families with the clear knowledge that boys and girls are supposed to be different, as obviously evident in physical appearance. The reaction to male/female difference and the belief systems that define these differences are culturally bound and individually interpreted.

Men and women look different both physically and biologically; in most societies, they occupy different roles. Traditionally, men go into the wild to hunt for food, and they carry weapons to guard their families. Women keep the hearth warm and care for their offspring.

In today's world, the same vague expectations still exist. Men carry the larger responsibility for being the breadwinner; while women, even if they work outside the home, have greater responsibility for taking care of the house and the children.

What seems to have changed is that the power dynamics between men and women have shifted radically. Women are no longer completely dependent on a man to take care of them. They have ventured into areas that were previously male-dominated. Men have also proven to be capable of caring for their offspring without a mother's assistance. In current times, the acceptance of equal capabilities between men and women is more prevalent if not fully embraced.

The development of sexual identity in some societies is closely related to the culture's dictates. In patriarchal societies, gender differences are clearly marked. Men and women coexist in subcultures. Roles and divisions of labor are defined explicitly. Deviations from the norm are subjected to severe consequences and punishment. These kinds of societies stifle individuality and creative growth. However, certain psychological comforts are experienced when definite expectations for behavior are very clear. The notions of "right" and "wrong" are less ambiguous.

When people from strict patriarchal societies immigrate to other cultures where women have more rights and are permitted to flourish and become expressive, they often experience feelings of displacement, loss of control, identity crisis, depression, and anxiety. There are many examples of cases wherein the dynamic between a man and woman is completely altered. When a woman from a patriarchal culture is suddenly able to work and be the primary or equal breadwinner, and if the man is reduced in stature to being dependent and powerless, significant psychological ramifications in the sexual roles occur.

In the same vein, when a strong capable woman marries a man from a patriarchal society and immigrates to his country, she will likely be restricted, demoted, and confined by the dictates of that culture. Shock to the identity is experienced by her need to reinvent herself as a means for survival. Whether the woman's psychology is able to cope with these changes is a matter of speculation.

The body's physical ability and biological limitations also contribute to the allocation of separate roles and labors to men and women. Although, in recent times, women have breached many of the boundaries that restricted their entry based on supposed physical limitations, there are still many powerful belief systems that emphasize physical separations and differences between the sexes. Men are still expected to use their superior muscle power for lifting heavier objects, and women are called upon to use their sensitivities for more delicate, nurturing ventures.

There are many other so-called differences that are understood and unconsciously accepted. Lately, however, even the best "understood" differences are more gray than black or white.

Generally, men and women have similar aspirations and identical basic psychological needs. Everyone wants recognition, love, understanding, safety, and success. The areas that characteristically reflect actual difference involve the ways in which these similar aspirations are achieved.

For instance, men measure their success by the amount of wealth they accumulate and the kind of vehicles they drive. Women measure their success by the kind of mate they marry, the homes they live in, and the kind of mothers they become. Men and women both like to feel close and warm toward the people they love. Women, however, achieve intimacy through conversation and affectionate touch. Men, on the other hand, bond closer when engaged in a mutual activity. In terms of communication, women like to share and explore feelings and disappointments. Men like problem solving and discussing subjects objectively. Men often experience listening to the disappointments of others as criticisms and judgments.

Men seem to be more comfortable sharing their vulnerabilities with women than with other men. The behaviors men exhibit between themselves seem to be more competitive, characterized by playful defensive/offensive banter, rather than by the exchange of feelings.

Men have the ability to separate their sexual needs from their emotional expression with some flexibility, while a woman's sexuality seems more tied to the expression of her feelings. This seems to be a major sore spot that generates many misunderstandings between men and women. A man's behavior in performing what he considers to be casual sex can be misinterpreted by the woman as an expression of devotion. A man can also misunderstand a woman's gestures toward sex. He may understand them to be a signal for having a good time, while her intentions may be toward deepening their relationship.

Divisions of labor are often disputed between couples. The general expectation is for women who don't work to conduct the business of managing the household and childrearing. Women who do work still feel compelled to carry the major responsibilities of the house and children. The "home" is usually considered to be the woman's territory, regardless of whether she has business outside of the "home." Men also assume that the territory of the household and children belongs primarily to the woman, whether she works or not. The "unfair divisions of labor" are often points of contention in couple's counseling.

In conducting psychotherapy, the individual is viewed and considered from every angle. How gender and its meanings are regarded depends primarily on an individual's psychological interpretations of their own sex and its implied role. Psychotherapy considers the patient's gender-role interpretation, and then explores how it fits in and relates to their life's choices and cultural settings. The struggles and incongruities that emerge direct the concerns of the therapeutic processes.

The perspective regarding gender that is useful for psychotherapy is to view the sexes as a continuum, rather than as two separate categories. This perspective acknowledges psychological and biological differences between men and women. However, the notion of the continuum reflects the fact that each person carries within themselves aspects that are male and female, as defined by the archetypes. The proportion and distribution of male and female energies varies based on the individual's self-concept and developed identity.

For example, a congruent and well-distributed proportion of male/female energies in a male would produce a strong, potent, and capable man who is also in touch with his vulnerabilities and is a caring, nurturing person. The caring, nurturing woman who is also able to be strong, potent, and effective in the world represents well-distributed male/female energy in a female. The appropriate balance of male/female energy in response to an individual's lifestyle is a concern for the psychotherapist to explore.

Conflicts arise when "strong" men who are powerful and successful in the world are cold, unavailable, self-centered, and controlling. This type of man is unable to sustain healthy relationships. The most likely candidates for being caught in partnership with this dynamic are meek, dominated, self-effacing, undeveloped, and victim-like individuals. This "strong" type of man has an overload of male energy and is not in touch with the female parts of his psyche. Helping him to discover the reasons for his imbalance and then finding the means to connect with his female energies softens the exterior masks, and allows for full access to all aspects of his inner psyche.

Women who struggle to be successful in the world but experience continuous failure may not be connected to their potent male energies. They have very warm, loving personalities, but cower easily when faced with the confrontations and battles of life. Understanding the reasons for the disproportion in their psyche's energies will introduce these women to possible paths toward balance. Achieving balance leads to potency and effectiveness, and the realization of active goals in the world outside of home.

A reversal of the proportions can also occur in both men and women. A man can be fully in touch with his female energies but unable to assert his needs and fight life's battles. He can be wounded and defeated when he ventures onto the playing field. This man needs to become more in touch with his male energies without losing the connection he already has to his female parts.

The woman who is labeled a "ballbuster" on life's battleground may have lost her connection to the female archetypes and be more connected to her male energies. This imbalance is seen when she doesn't exhibit any female softness and behaves in stereotypical sorts of male domination. To feel more whole and in touch with all aspects of the self, this woman also needs to find the balance between being female yet strong and capable in the world at large.

When imbalances between the distribution of male and female energies are present, there are also valid psychological reasons why they developed. It is important to understand the nature of any disproportion before embarking on a healing path to bring forward a more appropriate balance. Usually the reasons for the development of the psyche's various proportions relate back to an individual's survival needs and subsequent coping mechanisms. A lifestyle may have been created to accommodate these coping mechanisms and ensure their perpetuation. This could all have taken place on an unconscious level and become an automatic response. Whether these mechanisms or imbalances are still necessary for the person's survival and coping in their current life is a key question to explore and review in therapy. Other options and avenues for enhancing and updating the individual's self-concept can then become possible.

ରୋ ରୋ ରୋ

Case Study: Kathy and Peter

The following case study depicts the conflicts between couples that can arise pertaining to gender roles.

Kathy and Peter met in law school. Kathy was two years ahead of Peter in their studies when they married. While she worked, he stayed home to finish school and prepare for the bar exam. When she came home at night, Peter had a lovely meal prepared for them. Under Peter's care, the house was spic and span, and the laundry was all done. They were happy together and seemingly content with this arrangement. Kathy loved being taken care of. She was not an accomplished cook and hated housework.

After Peter completed his studies, passed the bar exam, and eventually found a good work position, the established routine at home became unclear. Peter and Kathy both worked hard and kept long hours. There was no longer anyone at home waiting to take care of them and their needs. To compensate, they either ate out or ordered take-out. The laundry piled up and dust settled everywhere. On weekends, they were both too exhausted from the grind of their week to do any housework. They used the time to relax, play a little, and recharge their energies. Neither Peter nor Kathy seemed willing to take the reins and manage the household. Outwardly, everything appeared to be fine; however there was a quiet Mexican standoff brewing between them. When the tension could no longer be contained, they were forced into having an open discussion.

Peter felt that he had paid his dues by being the "housewife" when Kathy was the sole breadwinner and supported him. He was grateful to Kathy but firmly believed that he had been forced into the role of "housewife" because of circumstances; he had complied in the name of fair play. Once he found work and was no longer dependent, he sought to regain his manhood and assert his role. He *could* cook and do housework well, as he had demonstrated, but he believed that this was the domain of the woman and beneath his male stature.

Kathy was shocked. She had no idea that Peter had felt demeaned when he took care of her. She had felt touched and even proud of him, and believed him to be a very modern man. She had no hint that his values as a man were so traditional and that he harbored resentments from their circumstances. Kathy was also outraged. She thought, with both of them working long, hard hours and bringing home equal pay, that they could at least divide the household duties.

Peter refused to take part in any division of labor at home. He reluctantly agreed to hire part-time help. Privately, he believed that hiring a housekeeper was a waste of money, since it would put a huge dent in their income. He thought that Kathy should cut back her hours at work and perform her "natural" duties as a woman taking care of their home. Kathy's career was important to her, and she declined that option. A distance grew between the couple. They both had to readjust to their new view of one another.

When the time came to have children, Kathy did take some time off work to give birth and be present for the babies during the first year of their growth. However, she resumed work at the end of the first year and had a fulltime nanny/housekeeper, despite the expense. During the time that she was a stay-at-home mom, Peter was the most content with the arrangement.

Peter spent only quality time with the children. He did not participate in their care or attend to their needs. He felt that he was paying the nanny/housekeeper to perform those duties. He was only helpful when Kathy was ill or had to travel for work. Otherwise, he was always busy and unavailable. Kathy had to undertake full supervision of the household and childrearing matters. On weekends, the nanny was off, and Kathy had the sole care of their two children.

Every time the division of labor came up for discussion, Peter's contention was that it was not a man's role to be involved in the care of the house and children. Kathy felt so extended with all her duties that she had no time for herself or her relationship with Peter. She felt disillusioned and was angry toward his "backward attitudes" about what he considered manly and what he expected a woman's role to be. It flabbergasted her. She thought that she had been fooled into marrying a stranger.

Their marital relationship suffered, and they grew more distant from each other. Their expectations of gender roles were so far apart that any reconciliation or compromise seemed farfetched. Their children were the glue that kept the semblance of the family intact.

ରଓଓର

Psychological Dynamics

Peter and Kathy were both strong, smart personalities. Whether they were consciously aware or not, they were engaged in a power struggle. The content of their dispute pertained to the differences between male and female roles and how these affected the division of labor in their relationship. Both seemed to exhibit a fair balance of male/female energies. There were underlying issues impacting their disagreements. The overt power struggle constituted the outer layer and was not the root of their problems. Their arguments about who was "right" and "more up to date" in terms of what was male versus female seem overplayed and a distraction from deeper wounds. That they were engaged in a battle of sorts was obvious; the subject of their engagement felt secondary.

It was not clear if either party wanted to surrender and/or capitulate. With surrender comes loss. In any dispute that impacts intimacy and human connection, there can be no winner or loser. If the ultimate goals are to be together, come closer, and grow more intimate with one another, then a mutually beneficial and peaceful resolution has to be discovered.

The primary direction of psychotherapy was first to confront the existence of the power struggle. Once acknowledged, the attempt to understand and grasp the deeper meanings of the dynamic could be put under consideration. Posing therapeutic questions opened the path toward that goal.

This couple had focused on the issue of the differences between male and female roles and had drawn opposing lines that kept the fight alive. This mode of operation caused distance and diminished intimacy between them. The questions posed involved exploring the purpose that these behaviors served. If they were disillusioned by their expectations of one another, could they still come to terms with the realities they had discovered and make peace?

From observing Peter's relentless, stubborn stance, it was likely that he may have suffered shame and some ego damage when he was dependent on Kathy's support. He made several derogatory statements regarding "playing the housewife."

His refusal to be involved in household matters was overstated and too strong. This indicated festering psychological wounds still alive in his system. Exploring the circumstances of that period in his life clarified his choices and redefined the "housewife" role. The shame that Peter experienced while performing feminine household chores could be transformed so that he could see that, instead, they reflected his ability to be versatile, caring and fair minded.

This change in attitude could reverse his sustained injury, and he could come to see his participation in household duties as commendable behavior. Helping Kathy to become more sensitive and empathic toward Peter's notions of his manhood, even if she disagreed with them, would lead her to soften her position toward him.

If the power struggle continued, it would eventually deteriorate their ability to come close to one another, and could eventually reach a point of no return. Raising their awareness that they were standing *against* each other rather than working *together* as partners also began to pave a way out of the power struggle dynamic.

The intrapersonal wounds—Kathy's disillusionment and Peter's shame—needed to be healed and reinterpreted in order to shift the focus to work on their interpersonal exchanges.

If the intention of their personal goals could be clarified, then conciliatory resolutions could be implemented to close the rifts in their relationship. If they remained strongly motivated to stay together, then they should be willing to participate in the work needed to keep their marriage alive, and to explore the personal growth that would help them overcome the challenges in their relationship.

CRCRCR

Veis Djalali

EXPRESSIONS OF SEXUAL BEHAVIORS

There are vast amounts of research and studies on human sexuality from both psychological and biological perspectives. Studies identify and divide sexual response into three stages: desire, arousal, and orgasm. Dysfunction can occur at each stage. Individuals can also be dysfunctional in more than one stage, and stages can overlap. Behavior Modification theorists have devised for sex therapists successful treatment plans for all of the stages and various varieties of sexual dysfunction.

This essay will not review sexual dysfunction and the concomitant treatment plans. The aim of this chapter is to explore and discuss sexual behaviors that can affect and/or cause psychological conflict and consequences. It focuses on those individuals who are not sexually impaired in terms of desire, arousal, or orgasm. These individuals are able to perform satisfactorily at all three levels. Situations, circumstances, and inclinations, however, play critical influences in guiding their sexual pleasure and successful outcomes.

Elaborate self-defense systems are often devised in order to safeguard an individual from getting hurt or experiencing disappointments. A common defense strategy is to compartmentalize and separate the mind from the body. In sexual expressions, this translates into the separation of sexual acts from feelings of love and attachment. Separating having sex from feeling love is supposed to safeguard an individual from being hurt and is thought to simplify the expressions of attachment. People with this defense strategy cannot love the object of their sexual attraction. They are also unable to experience pleasure, closeness, and gratification from having sex with people whom they love. People who have experienced major loss and trauma from past attachments are likely candidates to be susceptible to this syndrome. It is a self-protective defense mechanism designed to prevent painful experiences that may come with attachment.

Men in general profess to be able to have sex without love. They separate and compartmentalize sex from love, but they may not be affected so much that they have a complete inability to experience love and sex simultaneously.

Often this syndrome impacts marriages and long-term relationships. In relationships that are based on mutual love and caring, the person who has this syndrome is unable to perform satisfactory sex. In certain cases, no sex can be performed at all. The inclinations of an individual with this syndrome are to revere and idealize their love objects, placing them on a pedestal. Sexual experiences are only to be performed with people when there is no respect or caring. As a result, people who have this syndrome are often unfaithful, and have sexual encounters with people whom they cannot care for or tolerate. Obviously, their love partners are bound to be unhappy and unfulfilled, putting their relationship in jeopardy.

In literature, this syndrome is sometimes labeled as the **Madonna/Whore complex**, and refers primarily to men. However, separating sex from love is also prevalent among women, as well.

Treatment of this syndrome usually entails exploring the trauma and painful episodes that began to formulate this defense mechanism. Often primitive and childlike feelings are embedded in original wounds that have sustained and been perpetuated. Psychotherapy can help to heal these wounds. The goal is for the patient to develop mature perspectives regarding the complexities involved in relationships. Therapy can aid with the discovery of more effective self-protection mechanisms, ones that do not inhibit growth and wellbeing.

Sometimes sexual performance becomes habituated and ritualized so that successful outcomes can occur only in certain times or situations and only under specific circumstances. There are wide ranges of behavior that describe these particularities. A few of these circumstances will be discussed below, in order to exemplify the characteristics of these types of sexual expression.

There are individuals whose arousal and desire for sex can be stimulated only if **elements of danger** are involved. Disasters, catastrophes, awkward situations, public places, anticipation of being imminently discovered can all be aphrodisiacs and inspire arousal and desire. Ordinary, safe and comfortable situations will not activate the sexual drive for these individuals. It is said that Casanova may have had this condition; hence, in some studies, this particular state is referred to as the **Casanova Syndrome**.

Being in a relationship is hampered if the sex act can be performed only under dire circumstances. It is difficult to orchestrate events that will elicit the thrills and excitement of danger during the courses of everyday life. For these individuals, some event or events in their formative years led to this type of inclination. Usually, these individuals do not seek psychotherapy but tend to remain single and have serial sexual encounters.

Sexual expressions within specific and particular confines are deemed **fetishes**. Sometimes fetishes are used as an enhancement in a sexual exchange. At other times, fetishes become obsessions that are needed for a successful sexual act to take place. One example of a harmless fetish is when an individual wears an undergarment belonging to the opposite gender underneath their clothes throughout their workday; this fans the arousal and anticipation of the sexual act to come. An example of an obsessive and unpleasant fetish involves the need to urinate and defecate on a sexual partner in order to be aroused during the sexual experience.

Costumes, objects of any kind, certain areas of the body, body functions, and reenactments of childhood episodes can also become the focus for fetishes. Conflicts emerge between participants in the practice of a fetish primarily when mutual pleasure and consent has not been attained. When a fetish is forced upon a partner, it is no longer an arena for sex play. It becomes abuse.

In treatment, it is significant to understand the psychological meanings of a fetish within the individual's repertoire before devising a plan of action. Sometimes the narrative of the fetish is a descriptive blueprint of some psychological struggle.

The senses—sight, smell, touch, hearing, and the imagination—are the vehicles and means for enhanced pleasure during sexual interactions. Most people enjoy looking at naked bodies and watching others during sex play. If this were not the case, *Playboy* type magazines and the pornographic film industry would not be in business. Using the eyes in this regard is a kind of voyeurism, but it is not considered detrimental behavior.

When an individual can only be aroused sexually by watching someone else conduct a private act without his or her knowledge or consent, this individual is considered a voyeur from both a clinical and criminal perspective. For a voyeur, a good deal of their arousal and pleasure derives from the watched person's ignorance or lack of awareness of their being viewed.

Voyeurism is not a joint venture. It is a solo act, a form of masturbation that crosses over into criminal behavior. The voyeur is usually unable to perform sexually in a relationship, or if they are able to, their enjoyment of the behavior is minimal. Voyeurism becomes a form of obsession, one that drives the individual into compulsive behaviors.

In psychotherapy, voyeurism is connected with the issues of power, control, and the inability to share and connect with others. The exploration and understanding of these dynamics would constitute the therapeutic goals.

Some couples participate in ***group sex and ménages à trois***. If couples come to therapy as a result of such a venture, then it is likely that the incident had some negative consequences on the relationship dynamics. Couples need to have high levels of trust and a solid foundation in order to open the dyad for experimentation. Even though the venture may be exciting and arousing in the immediate sense, jealousies, feelings of betrayal, remorse, and competitive reactions may develop afterwards. Despite mutual agreements and resolves to play at this sort of sex games, a breakdown of trust between the couple can occur.

If a couple decides to try this path, it is best not to invite close friends or acquaintances to participate in group sex with them or the ménage à trois. More complications and hurtful episodes are likely to arise with friends than with strangers.

Some bisexuals report being the most fulfilled in ménages à trois encounters. In fact, their arousal and gratification are especially heightened during any sexual experience when both genders are present.

Inflicting pain, be it masochistic or sadistic, is usually part of various ritualistic exchanges during sexual expression. There are individuals who feel desire and arousal when anticipating and/or receiving pain. There are other individuals who are sexually aroused when they anticipate inflicting or do inflict pain on others. There are also people who are both masochistic and sadistic. High levels of control, ritual and costumes characterize S&M play. It is considered "play" because strict rules are applied when inflicting and receiving pain. Tolerance levels are predetermined and adhered to by mutual consent. A good deal of the gratification experienced is connected to the creation of these dramas, rituals, and playacts. Elements of danger and pushing the limits on the pain-toleration scale add spice to the experience. If the situation departs from the realm of play and crosses into reality, it becomes *torture* and *victimization*. Maintaining safe boundaries is a fundamental rule of this game.

Psychotherapy becomes relevant in these cases if the individual who practices **S&M** is unhappy and guilt-ridden from performing or participating in these acts. Practicing these behaviors has an addictive component. If individuals feel compelled and are driven toward this outlet, finding themselves unable to stop, then psychotherapy is advised. If spouses or partners become involved or are coerced into S&M practice, questions arise around the relationship dynamic, and abuse has to be considered. Spouses or partners can also object and be horrified by the discovery that people they love participate in S&M acts. In order for the behavior to stop, the compulsion's motivation has to be addressed.

There are wounds and psychological reasons that drive these behaviors. Secrecy and anonymity play a significant role in these rituals. Not many participants *seek* therapy for this compulsion. They are usually *forced* to come for therapy either by a loved one or a court order.

The psychology of the **pedophile** is complex. Most are locked in a childhood stage of development. Their bodies and intellects have matured, but their emotional development has not. Forming attachments and love connections with peers is very difficult for these individuals. Any relationship based on equality and mutual exchange has no meaning for the pedophiliac. Force, subjugation, and seduction mixed with subterfuge and control are the driving motivators of the sexual abuse of children.

Victimizing a child into submission under controlling circumstances, be it through seduction or rape, is an arousing element for these individuals. The naïveté of youth and the helplessness and vulnerability of children make them easy candidates for falling prey to the pedophile. Victimizing and controlling someone who might be dependent and much less powerful inspires the sexual arousal. Deep psychological disturbances guide and direct the motivations of the pedophile.

Since the acts are criminal, the Justice Department is primarily responsible for referring these individuals for psychotherapy and rehabilitation. There are pedophiles that experience shame and remorse about their compulsion. Therapy may help them to overcome their pathology. Child abusers can also be psychopaths and/or sociopaths who have no concept or understanding of the depravity and harm inflicted by their behavior. They are driven only by self-interest, and are not likely candidates for benefiting from psychotherapy.

Transvestites vary, and can be of either gender or sexual orientation. Cross-dressing is sometimes a fetish and an arousal factor. At other times, cross-dressing has more complex components.

When cross-dressing is practiced as a fetish for sexual arousal, it can be conducted as masturbatory or with a sexual partner. Undergarments of the opposite sex are commonly used to stimulate the imagination and fantasies in such practices. Some men seem to have a fascination with wearing stilettos, silk stockings, nail polish, and feminine makeup as enhancements for their arousal. Women have been known to gravitate toward men's boxers, butch haircuts, and whatever their imaginations consider to be rough, masculine garb in order to stimulate the arousal factors.

At times, men in powerful positions are driven to cross-dressing. By exchanging their masculine suits of armor for soft, clingy and flowing feminine garments, these men experience relief and become able to shed the characteristics that made them powerful and influential in their life's work. The literal act of cross-dressing allows these men to connect with the softer and less dominant aspects of their personalities. They are then able to relax and recharge before reverting back to their male dominant roles and clothes. These men's lives have little tolerance for softness and passivity. They have compartmentalized their personality into dominant and recessive components. A radical change, like cross-dressing, allows them to shift gears and experience the different ranges within their personality.

In other instances, wearing the clothes, paraphernalia and corresponding get-up of the opposite gender gives the wearer a sense of power and control. This sense of power is derived from daring expeditions into public arenas, where the cross-dresser displays him or herself and "fools" the people at large by their convincing transformation into a personification of the opposite sex. Their pleasure comes mostly in parading around and observing the reactions of shock and disbelief in others. This is a form of exhibitionism. An audience is required, and the reactions of spectators are paramount for the success of this adventure.

Psychotherapy becomes a factor for transvestites if it is voluntarily and they have some motivation to alter these behaviors. Sometimes, tangles with the law force a cross-dresser into therapy. There are more incidents of seeking therapy when spouses and partners of transvestites find cross-dressing to be incomprehensible and unacceptable behavior. It is very difficult to change this practice if the transvestite is not willing.

Transsexuals are of the firm belief that some biological error transpired in their prenatal physiological development. They view themselves as being trapped in the wrong body and assigned the wrong gender. Despite the look of their outer body, transsexuals internally identify with the opposite gender. Anxiety, depression, and psychological conflicts surround this gender misappropriation. The existing surgeries and hormone therapies that transform genders involve a lengthy and arduous process that requires patience and high motivation.

The issues that require psychotherapy along with these processes are numerous and continue throughout the adjustment period and transition. The impact that this transformation has on the transsexual's loved ones and family members is also intense and requires tending.

ෲൠൠൠ

Case Study: George

The following is a case study of a married military man who liked to cross-dress and participate in S&M rituals.

George grew up in a family of women. He was the youngest among four siblings. His older sisters doted on him but also teased him mercilessly. His father left when he was a baby and had no contact with the family. His mother did not like men. She dressed George as a girl and curled his hair into ringlets. She punished him severely if he exhibited any masculine traits.

As George reached puberty, his gender could no longer be denied. He was both tall and strong for his age. His mother was crestfallen and, for the most part, ignored or punished him intermittently. At the age of sixteen, George left home to join the military. He lied about his age in order to enlist. He could no longer tolerate living at home.

At the onset of psychotherapy, he was in his fifties and married to his second wife. He had two grown children from a previous marriage. His current wife owned a farm where she grew vegetables and fruit. George was adept with his chores around the farm and pitched in whenever he was home on leave.

George had begun to see a psychiatrist for medication. He felt depressed and anxious, and was afraid that his wife wanted a divorce. The psychiatrist referred them to couples' counseling.

In counseling George revealed that he had been leading a secret double life since he was a teenager. Whenever he felt anxious or overwhelmed, the only remedy that would bring him calm and peace of mind was for him to visit S&M clubs. He liked to dress in silk stockings, miniskirts, and stiletto heels, and be bound and dominated by a female. The designated dominatrix would force him to perform humiliating tasks and lightly flog him. After each episode, he felt invigorated, refreshed, and relaxed. He was then able to join and participate more fully at work and at home.

George's wife Nancy discovered a love letter that he had written to his dominatrix. She was devastated. When confronted, George confessed to the secret parts of his life, including his strong attachment to the dominatrix. The woman in question did not share the same feelings toward him, and had clearly disabused of his fantasy, telling him in no uncertain terms that what she did with him was strictly business, with no emotional attachment. She had returned his love letter and refused to work with him in any further rituals. He had been heartbroken.

His depression was primarily a result of the grief and loss of his dominatrix. He had whole-heartedly believed that he was special to her and that she cared for him. His anxieties were mounting, since he had refrained from going to the S&M club for relief, and not found an alternative outlet. He was afraid that his wife was also going to abandon him and dissolve their marriage.

His new resolve was to quit going to clubs altogether. He wanted his wife, Nancy, to accept him for who he was, including his inclinations. He also wanted to have occasional outings with his wife, dressed in his favorite feminine attire.

Nancy was a no-nonsense type of woman who found his cross-dressing incredulous and ridiculous. She could not imagine her strong, tall, handsome, masculine husband, who was also a good lover, being interested in wearing stiletto heels, wigs, and miniskirts. She was disgusted by his "foolish crush" with the dominatrix, whom she called "the hooker." She was still in shock about discovering his lifelong secret and infidelity; her outrage was in full bloom.

George was abashed by his own "stupidity" for falling for "the hooker" and jeopardizing his marriage. He reluctantly agreed to attend individual psychotherapy to explore the psychology of his need to cross-dress and receive pain. Couples counseling was also recommended. His agreeing to individual therapy was to appease his wife; George did not himself believe that he could ever change. He was more interested in finding ways to relieve his acute anxiety. He knew a sure-fire way to alleviate stress, but no longer wanted to go to the clubs, even though he could not imagine how he could stop wanting to go.

George's family background was an obvious blueprint and explanation for the S&M and cross-dressing behavior. His mother's refusal to see him as having a male gender, her regular punishments, his sisters' relentless teasing, and his choice of the military which is strict and male-dominated were the correlating foundations of his psychology. George was able to make the connections. He admitted that dressing up in female clothes came naturally. Being punished for being a boy was routine and expected in his childhood. He claimed that he couldn't fight off what had happened to him as a child, so he grew to enjoy it instead. Changing the enjoyment he has grown to derive from pain and cross-dressing felt like an impossible task.

ଔଔଔ

Psychological Dynamics

George was facing a number of intense psychological issues simultaneously. There were five or six major issues that overlapped and had life-changing ramifications. The first order for psychotherapy, depending on his ability to function in life, was crisis intervention.

George believed that he had been in love with his dominatrix. Her bold and final rejection left him grieving and suffering from heartbreak and loss.

The strict, male-dominated military life gave George some compensation from his male-deprived childhood. Yet he was unfulfilled. His cross-dressing into feminine clothes and the humiliating experiences imposed by the female dominatrix were reminiscent of his childhood existence and his relationship with a domineering, punishing mother. His anxiety in anticipation of being punished and then his relief after that punishment became an internal script that he obsessively played and replayed. George had habituated himself into believing that the only way to get rid of the overwhelming anxiety was to be dominated and punished. The post-punishment period became his time for rest, relaxation, comfort, and peace.

The heartbreak and deep humiliation he felt from the dominatrix's rejection became a real-life experience rather than something staged and play-acted. Experiencing this humiliation in real life altered a component in George's psyche. He could no longer allow himself to play at being humiliated: the real experience of humiliation was too unbearable. His decision to give-up the S&M play-acting, even though he craved it, put him in a quandary of not knowing how to alleviate the anxiety that gathered up within him. Helping George to find therapeutic and non-sexual means of relieving anxieties needed to be explored and implemented.

Another issue that George was grappling with was that he had finally revealed his secret life to Nancy. George was in new territory for the first time in his life. How he would handle his openness and the risks involved were to be discovered. The reactions of other people along with his own internal reactions needed to be fully digested and then refigured within both his self-concept and the projection of his persona.

George was also in the military. Revealing his double life to his wife and some close friends would not necessarily allow him also to be open at work. In fact, he lived in fear that his superiors would find out his secret and find ways to ostracize him or boot him out of the military.

His relationship with Nancy was up in the air as well. He had not had sexual intercourse with his dominatrix but had thought that he was in love. He may have even left Nancy if his partner in crime had acquiesced and had given him the slightest bit of encouragement. It was questionable whether he wanted to stay married to Nancy. Did he want to stay married because his supposed lover had rejected him? Were his feelings for Nancy and the life they had built together strong enough to continue and sustain the marriage? When he was able think more clearly, these questions had to be posed and clarified. Choosing to remain with Nancy out of a defeated experience with another lover was not a good foundation for the marriage to endure.

When the tension and urgency of the crisis subsided, Nancy and George had to decide independently if they wanted to be together and continue with their marriage. If they chose to stay together, there were many relationship issues that needed revision and boundaries that needed to be redrawn in order for new commitments to emerge.

George had betrayed the trust factor that existed between him and Nancy. He had had an ongoing secret life that he had hidden from his wife, and he had fallen in love with the dominatrix or "hooker." The ability to rebuild that broken trust was at the core of making any progress.

Nancy had also lost confidence in her own perceptions. She had been fooled by George and not seen through his cover-ups. Nancy was under the impression that George could somehow just snap out of his S&M and cross-dressing behaviors. She was either unaware or in denial of the complexities involved.

Regardless of Nancy's wishes, George really did not want to stop. He didn't believe that he could. He wanted Nancy to accept him as he was, and even join in, if she could, with some of his rituals.

Nancy's ability and willingness to expand her notions of "normality" so that it included behaviors that she abhorred in George had to be explored, revised, and modified. If she could not make room for his leanings, he would either go back into hiding, or the relationship could collapse. Nancy needed to weigh the strength of her feelings for George, since he might not be able or willing to change completely. Her decision to stay in the marriage could not be based on the contingency of his changing. He could most likely learn to modify and assert some control over his impulses. He was also self-aware and insightful. She needed to discover her own limitations and levels of acceptance.

Between George and Nancy, multifaceted issues were presented for psychotherapy. George's anxiety had to be leveled out first. He was in too much turmoil to be able to make sensible decisions. Both George and Nancy had to find the clarity of mind and heart to make independent choices regarding their commitment to their marriage.

Relationship counseling would not be effective and would not progress if the choices were still unclear and ambiguous. Nancy had to see whether she could accept George for who he was and not remain in a judgmental and critical position. If the S&M and cross-dressing behaviors were too much for her to bear, then being in a relationship with George would be difficult. If she could answer these questions in the positive, then marriage counseling could be attempted.

The prognosis for George to overcome the cross-dressing and S&M rituals was good. The primary hindrance was George's own reluctance. The fact that George could make the connection between his behavior and his upbringing was conducive for his taking strong steps toward recovery and developing different perspectives. He showed that he understood that his mother dressing him as a girl and punishing him for being a boy had laid the foundations for the S&M rituals and compulsion to cross-dress. If Nancy could come on board and be understanding and supportive, it would lend especially positive energy to the rebuilding of George's complex self-image.

Veis Djalali

"FOOD" AS SUBSTITUTE FOR DRUG, FRIEND, FOE AND/OR LOVER

Eating disorders have fundamental similarities with other addictive behaviors. All addictions are symptomatic, self-harming, structured defense mechanisms with chronic underlying psychological issues. People who gravitate toward food addictions have not been able to reconcile their need for love, recognition, and closeness in realistic and constructive modes of expression.

Other addictions like drugs and alcohol have denial and escapism at their core. Eating disorders are similar to other addictions in that they share the escape component to some degree. However, the patient who is suffering from an eating disorder has also given up the struggle of having their need for love met by other people. Those inclined toward eating disorders escape within themselves and devise methods to satiate their inner hunger for love, affection, and emotional needs, with food.

The obese person eats as much as possible whenever the need strikes and hoards food in the body. The anorexic is on a quest to transcend emotional needs by denying sustenance to their bodies. The bulimic is on an angry rampage to binge when the need strikes and then to purge in order to demonstrate the rejection of the need, thereby achieving control and freedom from wanting.

People with eating disorders all translate their emotional cravings and expectations into a focus on food as solace or culprit before allowing themselves to feel their psychological needs. Those who have eating disorders are at a loss when it comes to addressing their emotional hunger. Trauma, failure, and disappointment occur when attempting to conduct appropriate relationship connections with people and/or trying to confront anxiety and emotional discomfort. The level of pain is so high that further attempts are seen as impossible; the feelings become insurmountable.

Food is abundant, available, legal, and readily within reach of people living in affluent societies. The intake of food is usually pleasant and temporarily distracting. From infancy, taking sustenance has been used not only to nurture but also to comfort and give pleasure. It makes perfect and "logical" sense to feed when hungry. For people with eating disorders, emotional hunger gets confused with physical hunger. Whenever a discomfort of any kind sets in, feeding becomes the "normal" response, an alleviating mechanism to ward off the discomfort.

All addictive behaviors seek to numb pain and provide escape into an immediate oblivion. The drug of choice for those who have eating disorders is "food." Whether it is obsessively craved or fearfully rejected, in the life of those caught in this condition "food" replaces the primary need for relationships with others.

"Food" as a primary focus

Most people consider "food" as an object. To those with eating disorders, however, it is transformed and becomes a living, subjective, and consuming presence in their lives. "Food" becomes mother, father, friend, and lover, as well as an enemy and foe. "Food" replaces all of the needs and wants that an individual could expect from people involved in his or her life. The patient who has an eating disorder has retired from the arena of struggling to care and be cared for by others. She or he has withdrawn into an inner sanctum and closed the door on being wanting or vulnerable to the emotional touch of others. The needs all exist, lodged within the person and clamoring for attention, but are now experienced only as hunger for "food."

"Food," unlike a person, is always available in abundance, in variety, and at all hours.

"Food," unlike a person, does not reject or hurt, fall short and become unavailable.

"Food" can be consumed in volume: as much as the person wishes or has the capacity to handle. Immediate gratification, comfort, and pleasure are experienced with food. If disappointed, "food" can easily be discarded with minimum fuss. "Food" appears to have the means to appease a person's feeling of the anguish of emotional needs and wants that are buried deep inside the individual. "Food" alleviates pain and allows the "hungry person" to appear independent, self-reliant, and withdrawn. "Food" becomes an obsession in total control of the mind. All thoughts and objectives revolve around the decisions about what to eat and how to execute the venture. It is a consuming distraction. The importance of the rest of life fades into a shadowy background.

For people with eating disorders, "food" has a variety of personas. Depending on the psychological state of the individual, the persona assigned to the particular food transforms to express the feelings of the moment. The ritual of "food's" ingestion shifts in coordination with whether it is mother, father, friend, lover, or foe, and in respect to whatever relationship dynamics have already been formed.

Some of the archetypal examples are as follows: When food is "mother," the patient may need comfort, solace, and care. Soft and sweet foods are targeted. When food is "father," the patient may be struggling with solving a problem and therefore in need of something with caffeine that inspires and sharpens the senses. When food is a "friend," the patient may try to eat something new or adventurous and use food as a playful companion. When food is a "lover," the patient displays sexual intensity through flavors and different spices. When food is "foe," the patient creates a battle ground with crunchy, chewy, and brittle textures.

"Food" is also often used as an anesthetic, to numb the world into oblivion.

With over-consumption, some guilt is also present. The notions and perspectives of waste and self-obsession worm their way around the person's psyche, causing a vague awareness that an illness and/or disharmony exists. Unless the person with the eating disorder is interested in overcoming that illness and is motivated toward health, the guilt will become camouflaged and buried. Only a slight residue may remain in the psyche.

Obesity

People who consistently eat beyond capacity will eventually become obese. There are many deeply rooted underlying causes, which are similar to other eating disorders and addictive behaviors. The addiction to food can be as strong as addictions to drugs. When someone is afflicted, his or her need to eat becomes primary and dominates any other need, desire, aspiration, or concern. For those who are on the path to obesity, physical appearance, health issues, bodily discomforts, and negative reactions from others are all secondary and overshadowed by the need to fill their digestive track to capacity and beyond.

People who overeat to obesity seem to exhibit a careless regard toward their appearance and its effect on others. Weight has a positive meaning in the sense that it becomes security, protection, and armor against the world. The obese person views his or her bulk as a necessary protective shell, even though it may be ugly, uncomfortable, and cause health problems. Often, people who diet and lose a major portion of their bulk report feeling naked and exposed, and do not appreciate receiving unwanted attention from others. They quickly revert back to gaining weight if the psychology of their vulnerabilities has not been explored with some resolution. The psychological needs for this armor have to be identified in therapy, and then re-evaluated and internalized differently. Once the discoveries are understood, the obese person can successfully shed the weight and feel strong enough to live life in a vulnerable and exposed state.

The addiction to food is an entertaining obsession. Joy and fulfillment are associated with eating. The discomfort comes later. The obsession with deciding on and selecting food that is desired, purchasing it, preparing it and, finally, ingesting it, creates a euphoric state. Looking forward to the next feast is also in the forefront of the mind. Food becomes a 24/7 preoccupation.

When an obese person is in contact with society, they are usually avoided and/or ridiculed. The obese person exists in isolation, cocooned in layers of their favorite foods. No one can touch them. They are padded and unreachable. They conduct their lives with their armor intact. There are elements of depressed resignation and internalized defeat in the formation of this resolve. The obsession with food becomes a Band-Aid solution, protection from pain and hurt.

The obese person usually sees life's obstacles as dark and dangerous and charged with emotion. They require heavy-duty protection to withstand the inevitable hurts and potholes. Therapy needs to inspire the obese person to see and experience life from a different perspective. Exploration of the formation of their dark point of view usually reveals "the child" who never grew up to feel strong and capable. This "child" did not develop appropriate and adequate defenses, and has had unrealistic expectations of self, others, and life in general. The development of unrealistic expectations seems to be a major factor for everyone who has eating disorders.

૨૦૨૦૨

Case Study: Joann

The following is a case study of Joann, who has been obese since the age of twelve.

Joann was twenty-seven years old and obese. She had short, dark, cropped hair, swarthy olive skin, and a poor complexion. Her eyes were somewhat crossed, her gait was slow, and her head was set at a bent, sideways angle. Altogether she was unattractive and unkempt. The striking exception was her hands. They were beautifully manicured with fingernails painted a vibrant color.

Joann did not want to be in therapy but was forced to attend by her mother. She had a BA and had been unable to finish her MA in history. Mostly she stayed at home watching TV and munching. She was also a virgin.

As Joann's story unfolded, she described growing up in a family that was very social and high achieving. She was the eldest daughter. Her younger sister was very beautiful and slim; her baby brother was playful and lively. She was in awe of her father, a very successful businessman who was distant and uninvolved with family matters. She was afraid of her mother who "nagged and didn't leave her alone." Her mother wanted her to do plastic surgery, get her eyes fixed, go on a diet, and buy pretty clothes. Joann insisted that her weight problem was hormonal and not her fault.

Her sister was in ballet school and was a competitive gymnast. Her family was very proud of all her accomplishments. Joann used to be a gymnast as well, when she was younger and thin. She was also very good and had high potential, destined for competitions. However, she had a fall that resulted in a permanent back injury; this curtailed her gymnastic career. Her injury and the down time for recovery was the onset of her weight gain. Shortly after the incident, her sister entered the arena of gymnastics and came to excel at it.

Psychological Dynamics

It was obvious from this story that Joann's injury had traumatic impact on her emerging self-concept and self-esteem. It was as though a flame had been extinguished in her psyche. She gave up on developing a life that she could enjoy and be excited about. Her beautiful sister, usurping her gymnastic endeavor, added to her sense of defeat and failure. The only indicator of a spark that still held some energy in this sad tale was Joann's well-kept hands and painted fingernails. The vibrant color of her nails seemed to beckon for something more than her outward demeanor presented.

Further investigation revealed that Joann had a highly ambitious and competitive nature. She had grandiose fantasies of beauty and success. Her secret wishes were to be a model, an astronaut, a dancer, and even a swash-buckling pirate. It seemed that Joann's psychological development had frozen in her preteen stage. The injury that she sustained at age twelve coincided with this moment. Her aspirations reflected a childlike, preteen perspective.

The fantasies all depicted a physicality that was not realistic in light of the injuries she had sustained. Her denial of her limitations was glaring. Joann had never mourned or accepted her loss, or reconciled herself to the reality to which her injury had condemned her. Not understanding how to compensate and create other goals for herself, Joann had withdrawn into herself. She remained alone: lonely and anaesthetized by the relentless consumption of "food."

The subsequent goals for therapy were to rebuild Joann's self-esteem and to help her rediscover herself from a mature, adult perspective. Joann also needed to learn how to cope with loss, pain, and the happenstances of life in ways that were constructive and that enhanced learning. She needed to learn to look forward toward the future rather than dwell in the past.

Anorexia

People who suffer from anorexia behave more or less from the same psychological base as those who are obese. This base is rooted in some trauma that is experienced and then internalized along with misunderstandings and unrealistic expectations that perpetuate failure and disappointment around attaining desired goals. The characteristic coping mechanisms of the anorexic's response to those traumatic experiences, however, are the opposite of the obese person's.

While people who are obese need their body weight as armor and protection, anorexics embark on a quest to overcome and transcend the need for food. While food fulfills a variety of needs for people who are obese combined with some pleasure and gratification, anorexics are morbidly afraid to eat. Food is their nemesis. Food becomes the source and beguiler of all their problems. Avoiding food as much as possible is the mission of the anorexic.

The body image of the anorexic is altered to see normal flesh as fat. The grotesque thinness of the anorexic as perceived by others is not experienced or even seen by its sufferers. Self-denial and stubborn resolve are the driving forces in the psychology of an anorexic. Similar to religious fervor, the more the anorexic is able to resist temptation and the need to eat, the stronger is their self-righteous gratification. Anorexics often report feeling cleansed and purified by overcoming their biological need for food. There is a determined battle with nature at play. At times, the end result leads to death and/or severe damage to their health.

The concept of "food" has deeper meanings for the anorexic, as it does for the obese person. "Food" is symbolic of all wants and desires, loaded with emotional aches and pains. The symbolism is obvious and graphic. The anorexic at one time, usually in childhood, wanted and needed like everyone else. However, when denied and rejected a number of times, severe trauma was experienced. The trauma was not addressed nor healed; it is internalized and deeply embedded in the person's psyche. As a coping mechanism, the individual reinterprets and redefines "normal" wants and needs as weakness, negative, unsafe and too painful to feel. The anorexic individual is determined to abolish having feelings that suggest any desire that might render the person vulnerable. The consequent dictum becomes: "the less you want and need, the safer you will be and the more you will reduce the chances of being rejected." Anorexics live and conduct their lives by that motto. "Food" becomes the representation of all needs. Not needing to eat becomes proof of their transcendence of need. Their perpetual state of starvation is interpreted as victory and strength. The mind of the anorexic sees thinness as beauty. In fact, the thinner you are, the more beautiful in their eyes. Protruding bones and stick-like limbs are seen as accomplishments.

It is difficult to be in a relationship with an anorexic. They are also untouchable, similar to obese people. Self-denial is admired and even encouraged in certain value systems, cultures, and societies. Anorexics are masters of self-denial; its attainment creates in them a sense of confidence and control over all situations, their "logic" being that, if they can control and overcome their biological need for food, they can therefore control all needs and be safe.

Anorexics do not often seek psychotherapy. They are usually referred for therapy by physicians and/or because of a hospitalization. The physical damage to the body as the result of anorexia can be severe and sometimes life-threatening. Helping the anorexic to get in touch with their emotional and psychological needs is an arduous process. It usually requires a long-term commitment. Due to the life-threatening episodes that can occur, teamwork with other medical practitioners is necessary in working with anorexics. Mostly, inpatient facilities have the best-controlled and most comprehensive interventions for this condition.

CRCRCR

Case Study: Melanie

The following case study is a portrayal of Melanie and the history of her relationship with anorexia.

Melanie was a wispy, redheaded actress in her early thirties. She had been suffering from fainting spells, and her physician had insisted on psychotherapy. She lived with her boyfriend and believed that she had been anorexic since the age of eleven.

Her boyfriend was cognizant of her condition and had been urging her to get well. He wanted to have a family with her. She had not menstruated for the last decade.

Melanie's skin was translucent. She had an ethereal quality. She claimed that the camera loved her, but she had to lose ten pounds in order to feel more comfortable about her body.

She primarily ate lettuce and had an occasional tomato.

Melanie did not believe that she had a psychological disturbance but was worried about feeling dizzy and passing out. She stated that her relationship with boyfriend Keith was good. He traveled a lot and was not home much. She liked being left alone and having her space to herself. She preferred postponing making a family with him, as she wanted to concentrate on building her career.

Melanie loved being an actress. She declared that she felt free and unrestrained when she was in a performance. She could be whoever she wanted to be and could express herself in ways she would find abhorrent in real life. In "real life" she liked simplicity, order, and minimalism. On stage or in front of a camera, she could be profuse, untidy, complex, and abandoned.

Keith liked who she was at home. She could not understand his desire for children. To her, kids were messy and needy; having kids would alter their simple, problem-free life. She didn't believe that she would ever want to be a mother, in fact. She would only take it under consideration if Keith insisted.

Further investigation regarding Melanie's family of origin revealed that she was one of the middle children in a family of six. She had two older brothers and one younger sister. Her eldest brother and younger sister were her half-siblings. Linda, Melanie's mother, had lost her first husband in an auto accident. Chuck, her half-brother, was the product of that first marriage. She and her brother Greg had the same father. Their father abandoned the family when she was eleven and Greg was thirteen. Four years later, their mother married again and Hope was the sister from the third marriage. Melanie's strongest reference to her father was that, when he hugged her, he would call her his "little Miss Piggy."

Melanie's mother was a workaholic. She was never home. The children were left with the help and her grandmother, who had a significant role in their upbringing.

She fought with her brother Greg but always adored her half-brother Chuck. She tolerated her baby sister, Hope. It was her job to babysit frequently and she resented it.

Her relationship with her brother Chuck became more intense after her father's abandonment. Her father had a harsh and strict relationship with Chuck. He had at times punished Chuck by beating him on the bottom with a belt. On those occasions, Melanie had become very protective of Chuck, crawling into bed with him to soothe his wounds and comfort his hurt pride. She was nine at the time and Chuck was fourteen. Shortly after her father's departure, when she was eleven and Chuck was sixteen, they began a sexual exploration of each other's body that culminated in intercourse. An obsessive dependence developed between them. They had difficulties with being apart. Both her mother and grandmother were oblivious to the situation. Only Greg suspected something and threatened to tell on them. They bought his silence with bribes.

Their sexual relationship continued for the next two years. Finally, Melanie had the onset of her menstruation at the age of thirteen. Fear of pregnancy became a factor, and Greg's silence became more difficult to control once he turned fifteen and became more demanding.

In the middle of a family argument, Greg dropped the bomb. Linda finally became aware of what had been happening right under her nose for all these years. Chuck was then eighteen, and she banished him from the house. He enlisted in the military and disappeared from their lives.

Melanie, then thirteen, was ostracized and had no one close or attentive to her. Her father had left. Her brother/lover had been banished. She was betrayed by her other brother. Her mother was disgusted by her and was always at work. Her grandmother was hard of hearing and clueless. Her sister was a baby. No one liked her at school. She considered herself to be "chubby" with too many freckles and thought her hair was too red. She saw herself as a freak.

With this foundation at the start of her young life, Melanie withdrew into herself and shut the door on her needs and desires. Even though there had been some indications of anorexic behavior previously, she embarked on becoming fully committed to the practice of anorexia nervosa.

હ્રહ્રહ્ર

Psychological Dynamics

Melanie's relationship with her boyfriend, Keith, seemed to include some suspicious dynamics, almost replicating her family's scenario. He lived with her but was mostly absent, away and involved with his work. He was aware of her condition but didn't seem to be that concerned about her harming and abusing her body. On one level, he seemed to have replaced Melanie's distant and absent mother. On another level, he seemed to relate to her the way Chuck had. He had sex with a non-menstruating, childlike and skeletal body. They didn't seem to want much from each other. It was almost like a pretend relationship.

The healthiest aspect of Melanie's behavior was when she was on stage performing. There she came alive and appeared to be a full, three-dimensional person with wants, desires, aches, pains, and laughter. The irony was that she was only acting the part. In her "real" life, despite being in a relationship, she was isolated, alone and starving.

The goal of psychotherapy was to explore the possibility of using the acting experiences as rehearsals or a laboratory arena. The goal was to test out and experiment with actually feeling the emotions and involvement expressed in the scripts as a way of preparing for real-life experiences. Most of Melanie's belief systems were formed from the impact of trauma felt during her preteen years when she was still a child and had had no preparation. The stage was an arena that she knew well; she was comfortable there to let herself go, be spontaneous and emote. Literature is fraught with human emotions and follies that describe and teach fallibilities and wisdom. This seemed to be the safest and most meaningful path to inspire Melanie and to penetrate her hardcore defenses.

Melanie's distorted body image and phobic reactions to food were difficult to overcome. An appropriate, healthy body image had to be established first, before her mind would allow the fear of food and eating to dissipate. There are some innovative techniques with mirrors and videos that have successfully changed the body image of anorexic patients. Some work has also been done with the care and feeding of pets as a way to teach anorexics about healthy eating habits. All avenues were worth exploring in order to discover which methods made impact and inspired improvement.

In pursuing recovery with Melanie, a medical team had to be organized and within reach, in case of medical emergencies. However, the safest and most practical course of treatment for anorexic patients is usually an in-patient facility that has a team approach in place and the necessary staff.

Bulimia

The bulimic dynamic has components of both the obese and the anorexic characteristics. The bulimic orchestrates a cycle of binge/purge behaviors in rhythm with their consumption of food and whatever meaning that has for them. The urge to stuff the body to capacity and beyond arises during the "binge" episodes. The self-denial, cleansing and purification of the body and mind from needs and wants occur in the "purge" intervals.

The obsession with food and eating exists in all three states: the obese, the anorexic, and the bulimic. What is different for the bulimic is that it is very important to them to project a positive outward appearance of physical and psychological wellbeing. Therefore, it is more difficult to identify a bulimic person on the surface. They are not obese; their condition is not obvious on the outside. Nor are they skeletal, with tortured souls. For all intents and purposes, they appear to be attractive, healthy, well-functioning, and "normal" people. For the most part, bulimics live their lives in elaborate secrecy and subterfuge. Their addiction is hidden. It is only when they are on the road to recovery that they come out of the closet and their condition becomes more visible. These days, there is a good deal of awareness of people with eating disorders. People are much more knowledgeable about the signs and behaviors of bulimics. Those bulimics who are not ready to be identified have gone deeper into hiding and have learned how to counter the identifying signs of their condition with cleverer masking skills.

Previously, the key identifying behaviors were a disproportionate quantity of food consumed by a person who looked to be in good shape. Long intervals and disappearances to the toilet became a red flag for purging. An incessant focus on food and frenzy displayed when eating were other indications that someone was bulimic.

In recent times, however, bulimics have become aware that their behavior was suspicious and might reveal their secret. Therefore, elaborate counter-behaviors have been developed to further obscure the signs that might reveal their addiction.

The current practice of bulimics is to have two personas: one for the public's view and the other for their own private life. In public, "normal" eating behaviors are displayed; when at home and alone, full rein is given to binging and purging.

The "purge" is not limited to throwing up food that has been consumed. Bulimics are experts in finding many ways to rid themselves of calories, strategies that suit their personalities and circumstances. Spitting, over-exercise, and enemas are some of the other purging practices.

The psychology of the binge and purge syndrome depicts the dynamic of wanting, its painful impact, its denial, the cleansing and subsequent deprivation experienced. It is a vicious and all-consuming cycle. The bulimic has many overwhelming and passionate needs that cannot be fulfilled in a timely, sensible fashion. As a result, what they need and desire emotionally is translated into the "binge" of some desirable edible. The consumption of a feast feels like an orgy of the senses, even sexual in nature. When they are physically satiated, even though they are still psychologically hungry, they experience a great deal of discomfort, bloating, guilt, remorse, and self-disgust. They are then determined to rid themself of the guilty bulge; hence the purge activity becomes the next phase. To cleanse the self from needs and wants is as strong as the frantic wants that dominated the "binge" phase. After the "purge" has been accomplished, there is a euphoric period of feeling in control, in command, and even healthy. The third phase is when the feelings of deprivation, loss, and need set in. This leads back to the frantic hunger for food. The bulimic is once again propelled toward "binge" mode.

For the bulimic, this obsessive compulsion has an addictive, two-fold grip: the binge as well as the purge. Movement toward health and recovery become possible when disenchantment with the purge phase begins to appear. The first sign indicating recovery for the bulimic is when the need to purge loses its addictive powers while the need to binge still remains strong. The need to purge is reduced when the self-concept of the bulimic shifts, and the perception of self becomes more hopeful and positive.

When the cycle of the binge/purge syndrome no longer operates smoothly, the bulimic is faced with a dilemma that elevates their feelings of discomfort, anxiety, and confusion. The wants and needs exist overwhelmingly, yet the need and means to cleanse and purify have lost their hold. Therapeutic intervention is most effective and potent during this period, when the bulimic is at a major crossroad. They are certainly at risk of slipping back in to the binge/purge behavior or becoming either obese or anorexic. How they interpret and respond to getting "fat" is a major factor in how they move forward. A significant part of any intervention at this point is teaching the bulimic how to have some control and direction over their consumption of food.

"Food" needs to come to be seen as biological sustenance rather than as weighed down with emotional and psychological needs. Just like the anorexic and the obese person, the bulimic needs to be rehabilitated around the meaning and application of feeding.

ରୋରୋର

Case Study: Stanley

The following case study depicts Stanley's history and struggle with bulimia.

Stanley was a successful comedian and writer. He worked hard and was much liked and appreciated by his friends and family. He was quirky, talented, and seemed to enjoy his single life. He was a dutiful son to his aging parents and a wonderful uncle to the children of his siblings.

Stanley was forty-six years old and had been bulimic since he was twenty-five. He decided to become a bulimic when he overheard an ex-girlfriend refer to him as a "fat slob." He had been five to ten pounds overweight most of his life. Hearing that disparaging slur about his fat was devastating but did motivate him to never be fat again.

No one knew that he was a bulimic. On some level, he took pride in being able to eat whatever he wanted, knowing that he had the means to rid himself of the calories before it turned to fat. He lived his life by satisfying his inner hungers in secret.

Outwardly he appeared handsome, in good shape, accomplished, funny, and very likeable.

Stanley did not have a significant relationship. He had had occasional flings, but did not want to give up his independence, nor his privacy and his secret.

When Stanley began to fall asleep before purging or even to forget his purging practice, he became very fearful and anxious about gaining weight. The system he had implemented to control his weight while giving free rein to his desires, was no longer operating efficiently. His eating frenzy was acute but his purging became sluggish. He could not understand the change. He came to counseling for weight control.

Therapeutic intervention helped him to discover his intense need to be liked and admired, not only by his audiences but also by friends and family, as well. He found any negative feedback to be devastating and difficult to tolerate. He worked hard to perform his roles as the best son, brother, friend, writer, and comedian. He felt compelled to play all the parts perfectly so as not to be the object of any criticism. He obsessed endlessly if a review on one of his comedic endeavors was negative or not well received.

His mode of existence was to entertain, amuse, and give to everyone. On the other hand, to receive caring from others was problematic for Stanley. He made it very difficult for other people to get too close to him: he deflected the gestures by focusing attention back on them. He was good at listening to other people and helpful with problem solving. In this respect, he remained hidden and alone. He went home to take care of his needs for companionship and closeness by preparing and gorging on elaborate feasts. Then he promptly found the means to purge in order to remain thin, intact, and not needy.

ଔଔଔ

Psychological Dynamics

It was interesting that Stanley's need to purge began to diminish concurrent with the publication and success of a comedic book he had written on human foibles. Stanley was slowly feeling calmer and more at peace within himself. The acts and rituals of purging were becoming too time-consuming and irritating. He was also aging, and worried about the ramifications of the purges on his body. For the first time he was having fantasies of being a father and wanting a wife. These thoughts indicated that a shift had taken place in his self-concept. He was gaining psychological strength and feeling more centered and self-confident.

By acquiring some understanding of the psychological dynamics around what the binge/purge syndrome represented for him, Stanley was in position to struggle toward recovery. However, he was in a dilemma. While his need to purge was no longer powerful, his need to eat and binge remained strong. He was terrified that he would gain weight. In fact, his wants and desires regarding life had magnified. He was acutely aware of his internal hungers; but was at a loss as to how to attain satisfaction.

For the bulimic, the internalized emotional hunger floods their system. The force of this flood is similar to a hurricane: out of control and with destructive intensity. By comparison, it is relatively easy to appease this flood of hunger with feasts and the consumption of food. Calm and stability is quickly attained. To the bulimic, attempts to alleviate this flood of hunger in real life feels like an impossible task. Food, regarded as solace, is always immediately available, within the bulimic's control and difficult to resist. The "timing" factor for appeasing hunger is a major component of the bulimic syndrome.

The "timing" for the realization of goals and desires in life's process is precarious, unknown, and not immediate. The bulimic has a low tolerance and little patience for the wait time required between wanting and gratification. In order to recover, Stanley had to readjust, reinterpret, and separate his notions of emotional need from biological hunger. His perceptions of and reactions to feelings and needs had to be examined from a different perspective entirely. He had to learn methods of slowing his "timing" process for finding remedies and solutions. His acute response to disappointment, criticism, and any time his needs could not be met had to be reconsidered. Confidence in the self, endurance, patience, and achieving determination had to be reevaluated and relearned.

When the purge phase is no longer in place, some physical factors that emerge can become obstacles and impede the bulimic's recovery. The purge facilitates the bulimic's digestive track to hold low amounts of food for absorption. Bloating, water retention, and weight gain usually occur when the bulimic no longer purges.

Even with a lower intake of food, the bulimic's physical has to be reoriented and retrained to accommodate normal feeding practices. This inevitability may be too arduous for the bulimic and depress him or her to regress and slip back into the practice of purging. Fear of weight gain can cause anorexic tendencies and phobias and sometimes the sort of overindulgence that leads toward obesity.

For Stanley, limiting his food intake and dieting were a struggle, but he had a strong incentive to recover and become "normal." His physical and bodily discomforts were another deterrent, so he had to remind himself constantly that he had practiced bulimia for over twenty years, so his body needed time to become adjusted to "normal" eating habits. In his determination to become healthy, he actually undertook the attainment of a goal that required due diligence, pain, and no immediate gratification. The success and victory with that battle taught him some the tools he needed to recover from and control his bulimic tendencies.

CRCRCR

CRISIS? OR CATALYST FOR REINVENTION?

The state of crisis is a very broad term. It can include strong reactions to almost any situation. Intervention becomes necessary when an individual is overwhelmed by emotional reactions in an experience to such a degree that good judgment and their appropriate coping mechanisms are impaired. The therapeutic goals are to help the individual find realistic perspectives that help to transcend the flood of emotions and create movements toward appropriate, calm perceptions. The aim of therapy is not focused on deep work but rather on easing the crisis. This process varies by degree, depending on the individual's unique reactions and personal recovery time.

Experiencing crisis can bring forth the worst and the best in people. It is through action, not thought, that knowledge about the self can be concretely revealed. Behaviors and actions that are displayed during a crisis can be overpowering and transforming. Revelations can open doors for further self-discovery and provide material for future growth.

There are developmental stages in life that are natural hotbeds for potential crises. Crisis can also arise with life's normal happenstances. Some of the predicaments that can cause an individual to be in crisis include any kind of loss, illness or injury, the death of a loved one, divorce, an accident, being the victim of a crime or natural disaster like an earthquake, flood or fire, reactions to drugs, abuse, rape, war, a mass shooting, an unwanted pregnancy, abortion or miscarriage.

The crises that are commonly associated with the developmental stages of life usually occur at junctures and during the transition period just before the appearance of the next level of development. Examples of the transition states that are potentially conducive for an emergence of a reactive crisis are as follows:

The passage from childhood to the teenage years is usually fraught with emotion that is biologically based. Being in a continuous and highly emotional state, the teen is a ripe candidate for poor judgment. Often, the teen can be in the midst of difficult situations that could lead to crisis. Auto accidents, drug and alcohol abuse, sexual initiations and coercions, broken hearts, loss of friendships, out of control anger, depression, suicidal urges, and getting involved with committing crimes are some typical examples of these difficult situations.

Young adults experience a degree of crisis when they find themselves at a juncture where they must choose a direction in life that determines their future. Discovering and embarking on the "right" career path is usually anxiety provoking.

Leaving home and being on your own for the first time can be both exciting and frightening. If a young adult has not developed the psychological tools appropriate for this autonomous stride, then crisis can be experienced. Young adults are also in the process of choosing the "right" mate. This quest is often combined with heartache, disillusionment, disappointment, and loss.

The expectations and requirements of marriage can also put a person in crisis. Divorce and/or singlehood are conditions that include loss and feelings of failure that may lead to extreme reactions. Having children is sometimes characterized as a "moment of truth" for adults. It is one thing to desire a child and something entirely different when the full responsibility and care of a dependent human baby is at hand. Strengths and capabilities not previously recognized must be drawn upon in order to meet the obligations and requirements of parenthood.

Many parents restructure and redefine their identities to become parents. They build their lives around the needs of their children and the future plans they have for them. Once a child is grown and ready to fly away into the world, the couple's empty nest can generate separation anxiety and crisis for some parents. Again, redefining their identity and reassessing the demands of life without children to take care of becomes the task at hand. The empty nest is a natural, healthy, and inevitable phenomenon, but still can inspire a sense of loss.

Veis Djalali

Usually around the ages of forty to fifty years old, midlife crises can occur. This is a period when a psychological inventory takes place. Those who experience the midlife crisis question all of the choices that have led them to the present state of their life. Occupations, lifestyles, and spouses come under scrutiny. Grief and mourning for times and chances lost come to the forefront. Past hopeful aspirations of youth are revisited. There is a surge to recapture bygone times. Intense nostalgia and longing are experienced. Radical behaviors, depression, and anxiety are associated with midlife crisis. This juncture becomes a significant choosing point for the individual either to initiate the changes yearned for or to recommit to the life that is already in place. If the choices are explored with positive energy, then they discover a rejuvenating second chance at life. If their choices are taken with resignation and defeat, then psychotherapeutic intervention needs to take place.

Aging, illness, and the loss of vigor are difficult for most people to experience and accept. The strange dichotomy is that, while aging is underway, internally people feel as young and vital as ever. The body's diminishing strengths are realities that are difficult to dismiss. However, there is a stark disconnect between the body and the mind. The harsh reality of looking into a mirror and not recognizing the old person who looks back at you is experienced by most. The inevitability of more loss in the body's strength and function lurks in the near future. Death is around the corner and ever present in the consciousness. Some people devise elaborate defense strategies and undergo major plastic surgeries to deny and postpone the aging process. Panic attacks, other anxiety disorders, and depression become prevalent mental issues during old age.

As discussed, "normal" anxieties are experienced during the transition periods between developmental stages of life and these can trigger crises. However there are also moments in time, with the presence of adequate cognition, when the nature of existence comes into question. There is an internal jarring that puts reality out of focus.

For no particular tangible reason, the sense of self, the meaning of life, and the concept of the universe and time—past, present, and future—all become blurry and fluid. This state is referred to as ***existential crisis.*** The feelings that describe this state are similar to depictions of being adrift on a boat that has no motor or anchor marooned in the middle of the ocean. Or the feeling of weightlessness that is experienced when lost in space, without the pull of gravity. These existential crises are momentary episodes but have deep impacts on the psyche. Philosophers, religions, and social scientists have contemplated the questions and meanings of existence. There are extensive writings, studies, and literature on the subject.

The psychotherapeutic intervention in an existential crisis helps the individual to confront their realizations of "aloneness" and to understand that this is part of the human condition, as is undertaking the responsibility to be the architect of one's own life. Discovering that the decisions and choices made as regards one's attitudes and directions are within the individual's control can be profoundly positive and motivating. Understanding the consequences of the subsequent choices that are made is what constitutes reality and give meaning to life. This knowledge can be both powerful and frightening. The resolution to an existential crisis comes about when these responsibilities and choices are accepted consciously and with positive energy and resolve.

The happenstances in life that cause crises usually occur suddenly. There is always a shock and trauma component present. It is significant and advised to treat these traumas as soon as possible. If untreated, the trauma received will likely remain in the system in some form or other, and be re-experienced over and over as ***post-traumatic stress syndrome*** (PTS). Individuals respond and internalize trauma that results from an external crisis in a variety of ways.

Illness, depression, excessive fear, withdrawal, anxiety, obsessive reaction, drug and alcohol abuse, are all potential responses to an external crisis that individuals may experience. When a person is in the midst of experiencing trauma and reacting to a crisis, their behaviors are often erratic, impulsive, and overwrought with anxieties. The patient is often driven to make hasty, thoughtless decisions that can add to their stress factors. It is best to help alleviate the onslaught of emotions first, in order to allow the patient to gain some time and neutrality. As the patient becomes more grounded and develops some semblance of perspective, deeper therapeutic work can be implemented. The goals of therapy are to help to reorganize and redefine the traumatic crisis into a learning experience.

ର୍ଜ୍ଞର୍ଜ୍ଞ

Case Study: Lydia

This case study describes a person who was in a middle of a crisis and a candidate for psychotherapeutic intervention.

Lydia's physician referred her to therapy. She appeared to be a very pretty twenty-nine-year-old woman disguised in drab, loose sweatpants, a baseball cap, and old tennis shoes. She wore a neck brace. Her blonde hair seemed unwashed and hung in a greasy ponytail beneath her cap. She claimed that her boyfriend Jeff had "broken" her neck while they were having rough sex. Her doctor had x-rayed her neck and then prescribed pain medicine that made her sleepy. Despite the medicine, she was agitated and restless, having crying spells as she recounted her story.

Lydia and her boyfriend Jeff had been together for two-and-one-half years. Under his insistent pressure, she had undergone breast enlargement surgery and had removed all of her body hair with electrolysis. He would only allow her to wear tight, revealing clothes and be in full makeup at all times. He jokingly referred to her as his geisha. She did not enjoy their "sex play." He liked to slap her bottom and be rough. In this last episode, he had thrown her on the bed face down, had pressed her into the mattress, and had taken her from behind. He had pushed her head and neck down and held it at a strange angle. She had heard a crack and been in agonizing pain ever since. Ice compresses and aspirin had not helped. The next day she had called her doctor. The x-rays were inconclusive; no bones seemed broken. She was scheduled for an MRI.

Meanwhile, she was furious with her boyfriend and had refused to have further contact with him. She was considering a lawsuit. He did not express any remorse nor had he apologized. He was sorry that she had hurt herself but assumed no responsibility. He believed that she was a willing and active participant who enjoyed their "play." Lydia felt that she had lost all control and had been a mere puppet in his hands. She had wanted to please him and had been afraid that she would be abandoned if she denied his desires. This threat of his leaving if she did not comply was always present in their relationship. Lydia admitted to have been intimidated and overpowered by Jeff's personality. Lydia had no conscious awareness of seeing her participation and compliance as choices that she had made out of her fears of losing him. She saw herself as his victim. In "breaking" her neck, Jeff had become a criminal and had to pay for causing her injury. That was how she viewed the incident.

Lydia refused to clean up and be more presentable. She was afraid that if she showed her beauty in the slightest, she would fall prey to other men's lust. Her disgust toward Jeff had generalized to include all men and their "doglike natures." She was incognito, wearing disguises and purposely leaving herself unkempt in order to hide her beauty and vulnerability and to ward off men's attention. She wanted nothing to do with men and sex.

Lydia was also having difficulties sleeping and eating. She couldn't concentrate and focus at work. Her boss had been very supportive, allowing her to work from home at her own pace and time. She was flooded constantly with intense emotions. She cried with grief and raged simultaneously. Her friends stayed away, as they were tired of hearing her rant and rave. She talked incessantly and obsessively about her relationship with Jeff and repeated the details of the incident to no end.

Lydia's state of mind was chaotic. She wanted to get a breast reduction immediately in order to regain her original small size back. She wondered if she could become a lesbian and avoid men all together. She thought she might even convert to Catholicism and withdraw into a nunnery. She hated living in her apartment and yet was afraid to leave its doors. Everything in the apartment reminded her of her numerous encounters with Jeff. Any man who looked at her twice made her panic, as though afraid of an impending attack. She wanted to run away and hide somewhere safe. She wondered if she could be hospitalized, where she imagined she would be protected, however, she did not want to have any dealings with male doctors.

Lydia's senses of stability and good sense were out of focus. She displayed intense anxiety. She was beside herself with fear and had no idea how to proceed with her life. Being so overwhelmed with emotion and stress, she was incapable of making appropriate and thoughtful decisions. Therapeutic intervention allowed her to develop some perspective so that she could choose directions that would aid her in regaining equilibrium.

CRCRCR

Psychological Dynamics

Clearly Lydia was flooded with a variety of emotions that were overwhelming her system and not allowing her to make any sensible decisions. It was apparent that, during the course of her relationship with Jeff, she had capitulated to performing behaviors that went against her desires and wants. She had undergone breast enlargement, had removed all of her body hair, and indulged in rough sex play solely to please Jeff, and keep his attentions alive and ongoing. She saw her participation as something that she *had* to do, rather than as choices she had made for her own personal reasons.

Her need to keep Jeff attached to her came to an end when she sustained her neck injury. From that incident, she glimpsed a callousness and lack of regard in Jeff's behavior toward her that was difficult to deny. She felt fooled, betrayed, and brutalized by him. Denying or forgiving the behavior was no longer possible. She was shocked by the injury, enraged by Jeff's lack of caring, and grieved from the loss of the relationship.

There were also indications of self-blame in the mix. Lydia's unkempt appearance and the loose garments that disguised her beauty indicated some of the self-blame. It was as if she believed that her looks, her seductive body, and her enjoyment of sex were factors that contributed to her being hurt, injured, discounted, and not loved for herself. These thoughts and reactions were grounds for deep therapeutic intervention.

However Lydia, being in a state of crisis, was not able to comprehend or examine the psychology of her feelings. She first needed to get a handle on her emotions and feel grounded in order to prioritize the tasks at hand. Helping Lydia to identify and prioritize what was affecting her most and what needed to be confronted would start the development of attaining perspective. Linda's neck injury was the first obvious consideration to be confronted and dealt with.

As she pursued remedies for her physical injuries, there was psychological value in exploring the positive aspects of Lydia's behavior and reactions to the event. Lydia's self-esteem had been damaged; a positive build-up would help to balance the scale. It was significant to positively reinforce that she had found the courage and determination to leave a relationship that was not healthy for her. Even though she had complied with Jeff's coercions and felt dominated and victimized by him, she had had the strength to leave and stop the cycle after feeling abused. Once Lydia connected to the strength within her that had given her the impetus to stop being in an unhealthy relationship, she was ready for the next step in trying to understand the dynamics of her crisis.

The major components of Lydia's immediate crisis were the shock sustained from the injury itself; the realization of Jeff's lack of true regard for her; the actual loss of the relationship; and a number of issues that comprised self-blaming. Therapy divided the components into separate issues to be dealt with one-by-one. These components all rolled up into one ball were amorphous, overpowering, and lacked clarity, which added to her feelings of helplessness. When Lydia was able to see and deal with each component separately, she was on the road to gaining therapeutic resolution.

When the intensity of the emotions in a crisis subside, the opportunity for deeper therapeutic intervention becomes more likely. This crisis brought forth some of the psychological issues that had been previously hidden from Lydia's consciousness. She had been locked in an unhappy relationship because she had fears of being left. The abandonment fears in her psyche had been so strong that, in order to keep her attachment, she had participated in acts she did not want to perform. Exploring the roots of her abandonment issues allowed Lydia to have better self-understanding and discover the reasons for her capitulating behaviors. These understandings alleviated some of the self-blame and helped her to have more respect for the complexities of her needs and their ramifications.

She had seen herself as a weak victim with Jeff. If she could also consider herself as someone who complied but had been directed by her own motives as well, it would point out that she had not been a mere puppet. A good number of Lydia's reactions stemmed from self-debasement and self-punishment. Lydia had to come to realize that her beauty and sexual allure were positive attributes. She could control to some extent how she projected her beauty into the world, and could become more aware of its impacts. However, she was not responsible for how other people behaved and responded to her attractiveness. She could choose and select her responses to overtures. It would reflect growth if her responses to being found attractive were based on sensible understandings rather than on fear or the need to be loved.

Lydia had several other issues to be considered in psychotherapy. She was unable to accept that someone could love her for herself. Obviously, her opinions of herself had at one time been severely damaged. She operated under the assumption that, in order to get love and hold on to it, she had to perform and please. She had assumed that if she allowed Jeff to use her as a sex object or sex toy, she would win his heart. Investigating whether she had a history of operating with this personal myth was useful. Where had she first learned that she needed to perform before she could be loved? This belief may have begun in her family of origin and had become counterproductive. It merely perpetuated the dictum of the internal script. Lydia unconsciously chose people and situations that proved her myths accurate; as a result, she continued to feel unloved.

The exchanges of love are usually based on mutual respect and expressions of caring for the other. Objectifying the self is demeaning to both the objectified person as well as the perpetrator. Offering the self as an object to be played with often results in the gift being devalued. Helping Lydia to learn and understand that she needed to value herself and care about who she was before she could find success in the give and take of love was a therapeutic task to be undertaken. The obstacles and the reasons for her inability to value and care for herself in the past had to be worked through.

Lydia had learned to use her physical beauty to capture male attention. Yet she did not display any respect or joy in her body and its allure. The dichotomy was that she was also brokenhearted, believing that *only* her physical beauty could attract male attention; she—her unique person—did not count and was not seen. This cynical and dark belief system was similar to other myths in Lydia's psychology. The notion centered on the same theme that Lydia was not loveable for her inner self. She was desired only if she was pretty, sexy, and pliable. These beliefs seemed to be buried and embedded in her psychology and were most likely based in her childhood or early growing-up years of development. Some sort of sexual abuse in childhood may exist in Lydia's history. Exploring and recovering childhood learning and memories would be significant.

The crisis Lydia had experienced was devastating. However, it could be a catalyst that provided her opportunities to explore and examine deep personal myths that were, though buried in her past, controlling her present choices and behaviors. Further psychotherapeutic intervention would enable Lydia to find release from the depressed and suppressed outlook that made up her narrative of the past. The goals of therapy were to raise Lydia's self-esteem and confidence, and to strengthen her sense of self. If she could learn to appreciate and value herself, she would be in a position to select partners who truly cared for her, and who loved and appreciated her for who she really was.

ଓଓଓଓ

Veis Djalali

THE GROUP AS MICROCOSM

Group therapy creates a mini-arena where the social dynamics between humans are played out vividly and potently. Groups have emerging processes. Roles, status, and hierarchies gradually take form in order to command, rule, follow and discriminate. Partnerships and alliances are developed. Lines are drawn and group participants choose sides that are consistent with the roles they played in their families of origin, workplaces and communities. Communication issues and misunderstandings also appear in group therapy. These miscommunications are also consistent with the idiosyncratic miscommunications that an individual encounters in real life.

For the individual, the group becomes a microcosm of the world they inhabit. The roles that are adopted in group therapy had their origins in the individual's family's dynamic.

For example, a child learns to assume the role of a giver or taker in his or her family of origin during the early years of development. The same role will be personified as a theme in their behavior throughout the individual's life. This role will also manifest in the group's therapeutic process.

It is primarily in experience that the nature of the personality is discovered. Group therapy provides interactions with others and creates experiential episodes whereby the discovery of the self becomes evident and immediately observed. A skilled group psychotherapist will be able to orchestrate experiences and directions for the group's process to deepen in order for participants to better understand the self as an individual and the roles that the self plays in the social dynamics of life. The group also becomes a safe place and a laboratory to practice and develop new communication skills and discard obstacles in behavior that has prevented growth and learning.

Implementing ground rules from the onset promotes a safe environment for the members of group therapy. The commonly used ground rules are basic; they should be discussed and agreed upon during the first session. They are as follows:

1. **Commitment to attendance**: it is important to have an agreement on attending all the sessions for the designated duration of the group.

2. **Confidentiality:** nothing said or experienced in the group sessions are to be discussed outside of the group or with anyone who is not the group's member.

3. **Respect:** common courtesies are to be observed in the group. It is important not to interrupt one another and to give each other adequate time to share and express confidences.

4. **Authenticity:** it is crucial to be committed to being honest and authentic in self-revelations and in feedback that is offered to the other members.

5. **Outside formations:** the consensual agreement not to form private relationships with one another outside of the group's process. If members are attracted to one another, it's important to express those feelings in group, and refrain from meeting outside of the group for the duration of the therapy.

The rules can be revisited, modified, and changed in accordance with requests and subsequent developments. It is important to discuss the rules openly and adapt them to the group's goals.

There are many different types of group therapies. Besides therapy groups formed for the development of positive mental health, there are also theme groups formed with a specific focus, like: women's or men's groups; grief groups; divorced groups; multifamily groups; and addiction groups. Most groups meet at designated times and have designated durations. Open-ended therapy groups also exist, where participants come and go. All groups, however—be it therapy groups, a support group or a business group—seem to have similar stages of development and dynamics.

The stages that occur in groups are as follows. At the beginning, there is a milling around period, where the members get acquainted and take the measure of one another. Gradually, roles emerge, and lines and divisions appear. Members may form sub-groups. After the hierarchies have been established and the tensions for power and control have subsided, the therapeutic work begins to deepen. Members start to connect with one another and find common ground in the struggles of the human condition. Mutual feelings and experiences draw the members closer. Group cohesion emerges that bonds all the members into a union. This bonding creates warmth, comfort and support. At this point, the group has become a safe place for the members to be eager to share openly their innermost issues with trust and have positive faith in the therapeutic outcomes.

It is remarkable that in almost all groups of any kind, the same common roles emerge in the interactive processes between its members. These inevitable and identifiable roles are: the leader, the co-leader, the star, the outlaw, the rescuer, the joker or clown, the person most disliked; the rest are followers.

The leader is usually the designated therapist. Some therapists work with a partner or an assistant. The assistant is often an intern in training. The group psychotherapist has a built-in position of leadership, but does not become the true leader until he or she has passed the tests imposed by the group members to evaluate those strengths and skills that would command their respect.

The position of leader is a precarious one. The leader is part of the group, but also remains outside of the group to observe and intervene when necessary. The group members expect the leader to be mother, father, teacher, and protector. At each juncture of the group's process, the leadership's competence is questioned and reviewed, if not overtly then definitely covertly. The position of leader is never safe.

Respect for the leader has to be earned continuously with every event.

The relationship of the group members to the leader is usually ambiguous. While group members will compete to be close and special to the leader, they will also look for opportunities to de-throne the leader from the control position. Some members will have issues with authority figures and will be involved in antagonistic dynamics, challenging the leader at every turn. If the leader is attracted to or especially sympathetic or close with any member of the group, the others will view it as a betrayal. This will also not bode well for the person who is the object of any special notice. It is important for the skilled therapist to project an impartial, fair-minded and objective care for every member of the group and in equal measure.

If a partner with equal power and credentials shares the leadership position, the group members will have favorites and will attempt to align themselves with one or the other. There will also be maneuvers attempted to play one therapist against the other. Keeping the partnership between the leaders intact and harmonious has positive impact on the group's progress and becomes yet another test to pass in order to prove good leadership.

Most members have covert disdain for the assistant to the leader. The assistant is usually a student in training and is not in the position to claim honor and respect. The position second to the leader, occupied by the assistant, is envied and coveted by the others. The assistant's closeness to the leader is a cause for objection, as well. There will most likely be attempts to sabotage the efforts of the assistant to be useful and effective. Vying for the position that the assistant occupies becomes one of the primary agendas for all other members of the group. In order for the assistant to win respect, a strong enduring personality has to be projected. The assistant needs to demonstrate originality and separateness from the leader, and yet be harmonious and work in partnership with the leader in the therapeutic endeavors.

The person who is naturally popular and liked by everyone usually takes on the "star" role. He or she may not be particularly insightful or intelligent in his or her contributions to the group but still has impact and followers. Usually the stars are charming, attractive people. If the star supports the group's leaders, there is less dissonance and fewer competitive attempts to undermine and sabotage the leaders. It is important for the leader to win the star's support without appearing to favor or create an alliance with the star.

The person who makes every effort to break or challenge the rules of the group usually becomes the "outlaw." The outlaw's mission is to demonstrate that they do not follow or adhere to any dictums; also, that they are not interested in the position of leadership. They will not conform to any agreement. They proclaim to be different and their differences are their badges of honor.

The person who tries to nurture and help everyone out of difficult circumstances assumes the "rescuer" role. The rescuer is driven to be nice. Sometimes the caring that they express is profound, justified, and therapeutic. At other times, however, the rescuer's attempts to be helpful are inappropriate and tend to keep the group's therapeutic depths at superficial levels. The people who want to rescue are often not comfortable with intense expressions of pain and strong feelings.

The "joker" or "clown" can also play a role in trying to dissipate any strong feelings and anxieties that are expressed. Their attempts are done through humor and fun and can sometimes be appropriate and have therapeutic value. But they can also be disruptive and sabotage efforts toward deeper understandings, realizations, and growth.

There is always someone in any group who is disliked the most by the other members. This person occupies the lowest position in the group's hierarchy. They are discounted, discriminated against, and dismissed by most group members. This individual's reactions can either reinforce or justify the discrimination or cause division and discourse within the dynamic. Battle lines between members can support or oppose the individual who is being discriminated against. The role that the leaders take in these instances is very significant in the creation of therapeutic resolutions and in providing the learning of new behaviors.

The other members of the group fall in the category of "follower." They blow in different directions and support different causes, depending on the moods and dominant factors of the group's ebb and flow. They give mass to the majority rule. Their convictions are neither solid nor idealistically driven.

These roles are not black or white in their construction. They also often merge. The star can also be the outlaw or the joker or the rescuer. The outlaw can be the person who is most disliked. Each group develops its own particular character.

Group therapy can provide profound learning experiences and enhance communication skills. Skilled psychotherapists can offer safety for the group, so it is used as an arena and a live laboratory. The goals are to practice and experiment with new behaviors and find appropriate uses for effective communication.

ೞೞೞೞ

Case Study: Women's Support Group

The following case study described selected sections from a women's support group. The selections depict and highlight an event that is not necessarily typical, but does happen on occasion.

Seven women agreed to participate in a women's support group. These women had all been in individual psychotherapy with the same clinician for a while. They did not know one another and had not met previously. The therapist had offered group therapy to them as a way to enhance their learning better communication skills. They all had established their own individual closeness and trust with the psychotherapist.

There was no co-leader assigned for this group. The women were Laurie, Mona, Sarah, Sharon, Claire, Bonnie, and Patty.

Laurie was a graduate student in psychology. She was also the sole proprietor of a crime scene cleaning business. She was single, twenty-eight years old and originally from England.

Mona was a thirty-two-year-old attorney in a relationship with a married man. She was feeling her age and was frantic to meet someone she could marry and have children with.

Sarah was a twenty-nine-year-old artist, an only child who was supported primarily by her parents. She lived on the top story of a duplex apartment, while her parents lived on the first level. She dated and was waiting to find a forever relationship that was similar to the one that her parents enjoyed.

Sharon was thirty years old and a dental hygienist. Her husband was a dentist from India. They had a small baby. She identified herself as a hoarder and had difficulty throwing anything away.

Claire was a T.V. producer. She was twenty-nine years old and loved her job. She dated frequently but had not found Mr. Right. Her parents were pressuring her to settle down.

Bonnie was also in show business. She edited films. She was thirty-two and lived with a boyfriend but had some serious sexual problems.

Patty was twenty-nine years old and a kindergarten teacher. She was dating two men that she loved equally and was not able to let go of either. The boyfriends did not know they were sharing her. Her juggling act was causing her many anxieties.

The first two group sessions were low key. The participants got acquainted and took one another's measure. During the first session, the ground rules were presented. There were some objections as regards refraining from establishing connections outside of the group's experiences. The women wanted to be able to call on one another and have private time. This was discouraged. Finally everyone agreed to respect the rule and allow some time for the group to develop its own character.

With the help of the therapist, the goals for the group were narrowed down to a consensus. The group was to operate as a source of support for one another and help with congruency in communication. Clarifying intentions, expressing them congruently, and implementing the intentions in actions were the goals considered in the development of constructive communications.

By the third session, alignments were occurring among the group members. Bonnie and Claire were in show business, so they formed an alliance quickly. Sarah and Patty seemed attracted to each other. Mona and Laurie eyed one another initially. But Mona drifted toward Bonnie and Claire. Mona was generally liked and admired by everyone. She came across as astute and insightful. Laurie and Sharon stood alone. Laurie had a chip on her shoulder and was critical and judgmental in her remarks. She had a hostile and offensive stance. She admonished Mona for being involved with a married man. She criticized Patty for two-timing the men she was involved with. She made fun of Sharon's hoarding habits. She ridiculed Sarah for being financially supported by her parents. It was clear that she made everyone uncomfortable and afraid to share. Sharon seemed quiet and generally nervous; she wanted to be nice and please everyone. She spoke so softly that she had to be asked to repeat herself.

The psychotherapist had the given position of leadership. Since individual relationships with each participant had been established previously, respect and trust already existed. The discomforts displayed toward the therapist were fears of favoritism for some specific member. The participants carefully observed the therapist's behavior for indications of any special closeness between the therapist and the individual members. The group was testing the therapist's abilities to play fair and be equally attentive and caring to all. Treading consciously was the intention of the therapist in this regard.

By the fourth session, baby steps were being taken to share significant issues and to test the levels of trust. Bonnie was the brave soul who first opened up by sharing her difficulties in performing sexual intercourse. Even though she had lived with a boyfriend for the past nine months, Bonnie had not been able to have sexual intercourse with him. In fact, at the age of thirty-two she was still technically a virgin. She could participate and perform anything sexually imaginable but could not allow penetration. She was morbidly afraid of experiencing the anticipated pain of tearing her hymen. She believed that her fears were caused by several painful and difficult surgeries she had undergone in childhood. She assumed that her fears were directly connected to the open wounds left from the surgeries and the painful recoveries she had experienced.

The therapist felt that more exploration was necessary. Bonnie had come from a strict and religious background. She also exhibited the need to control and direct situations. These could also contribute to Bonnie's phobic reaction to losing her virginity. The loss of virginity could be symbolic for letting go and ultimately "losing" control.

Except for Laurie, the group members were understanding and supportive. They also shared their experiences and fears with losing their virginity and reaction to pain. Mona offered a solution. She had read about a treatment of using Botox injections on the vagina to relax the organ and make penetration easier.

Laurie smirked and made fun of Bonnie's having a boyfriend and, at thirty-two, still being a virgin and a chicken. The therapist had to intervene at this point to confront and question Laurie's hostile attitudes. It became apparent that Laurie found the group experience intimidating and did not like to share the therapist's attention with the others. She did not want to admit to being vulnerable. Instead, she defended and attacked. She thought that being a psychology student made her superior to the others and their plights. She was very angry with the therapist for not recognizing her worth and for expecting her to interact with people whom she regarded as beneath her level of expertise. She wanted to align herself with the therapist and co-lead the group. She did not want to be a mere member.

Mona asked her why she attended the meetings when she felt so out of place. Her answers were convoluted, without making much sense. The prevalent theme was that she was not a quitter. The therapist made several attempts to help Laurie carve a comfortable space for herself within the group, to participate as a member and to have the opportunity to gain value from the experience. The attempts were violently rejected. Laurie's reactions escalated into being disruptive, antagonistic, and hurtful. It became clear to the therapist that for the sake of the group's ability to progress and find trust, Laurie had to be asked to leave. She had not been ready for group psychotherapy. Continuing with individual therapy was more appropriate for her.

An individual session with Laurie helped the therapist to better understand her pain and difficulty with the group experience. Laurie's reactions in that session were gleeful and uncooperative. Finally the therapist concurred that participating in group therapy had been an inappropriate choice for her. She was asked to leave but given the option of one last meeting to say goodbye to the other members. She was also welcomed to continue in individual therapy with the clinician. Laurie became outraged, uttering a string of profanities. She declined both options and declared that the therapist was the worst clinician she had ever met and that she was doing well to be rid of them all. She emphatically stressed that this was not the end. She was going to report being thrown out to the licensing board; the therapist should expect severe reprimand.

After Laurie's departure, the group had to reorganize, react to the departure individually, and re-bond to form a new perspective. Though Laurie's presence was an irritant to the group's dynamic, she served a purpose. She caused many distractions and made herself the focal point. As long as she caused chaos, she dissipated the depth that could be achieved and the group maintained a homeostasis that prevented therapeutic growth. Laurie's departure opened up the potential for the group to become more cohesive and to have deeper aspirations.

ଔଔଔ

Psychological Dynamics

It is most difficult for any psychotherapist to dissolve a therapeutic relationship with deliberate purpose. Therapists usually value the struggles and processes of self-discovery in the therapeutic journey. Having the commitment and patience to be with an individual's struggle is an understood expectation between patient and therapist. Positive change occurs when the variety of choices is clarified and a patient is able to choose the path best suited for their lives. Imposing an unwanted choice on a patient for the good of the group is a difficult task. It is common for group members to compete for attention. The way that this attention is gained depends on the psychology of the individual.

Laurie vied for attention by being contrary, defensive, critical, and hostile. Numerous times she broke the rules of the group's contract that were set during the first session. She crossed the line of no return when her attacks on Bonnie became vicious and counterproductive. Her behavior forced the therapist to intervene and take Bonnie's side. Choosing sides was not the therapist's preference. Asking Laurie to leave alleviated the unnecessary negativity that her presence generated, but her departure also left an impact on the group's process. Losing a group member, no matter how negative the presence, leaves an irreplaceable void. Clearly Laurie had identified her role in the group as the "outlaw" and the "person most disliked." After her departure, there was an opening for someone else to assume those roles.

Mona became the "star" as well as the "rescuer" in the group. She was generally liked, respected, and delivered helpful suggestions.

Laurie was jealous of Mona's popularity. Since she couldn't be likeable, she assumed the opposite role of being the most disliked. Mona's helpful suggestions gave her influence and brought her closer to being identified as a natural co-leader. Laurie wanted that position and had believed that being a psychology student gave her the right to it automatically. Hence, the battle lines were drawn in Laurie's perception.

It is complex when a therapist invites patients from his or her private practice who are engaged in individual therapy to participate in a group experience. Group dynamics are similar to the dynamics of family structures. In families, the children compete for the position of being the most favored. Patients in group therapy also have the tendency to assume that the therapist belongs solely to them. Each patient wants to be the favorite and most special to the therapist.

Selecting group members from a therapist's private practice has the advantage of knowing the participants. It also extends their psychotherapy into another arena. The group experience enables encounters and relationship bonds that can be experientially observed and directly worked upon. A group can provide its members with a positive laboratory experience in which to discard old behaviors that no longer have meaning and to learn, acquire, and practice new behaviors. The disadvantage of having members from a therapist's individual psychotherapy pool is the potential for rivalries, competition, and jealousies similar to the sibling dynamics of a family structure. This transference can be therapeutically powerful and enlightening, but it can also be hazardous and fail, as in the case with Laurie.

Laurie could not tolerate sharing her therapist with the other group members. In her family of origin, her parents had divorced and remarried spouses who had other children from previous marriages. They also created more children. Laurie had been compelled to share her space and her parents with a number of half and stepsiblings whom she resented and disliked. She did not feel that she belonged in either family. She had left home as soon as she was of age carrying a lot of unresolved baggage. She had never been able to join in any group ever since.

By inviting her to be a member of group therapy, the therapist had hoped to create a positive sharing experience for her, and work on her issues more directly. Unfortunately, Laurie had not been ready for the experience, and the therapist had misjudged the "timing." Laurie managed to replay her internal script of being the outcast in a group. She had felt unwanted in her family of origin; being rejected from the group reinforced her damaged perceptions and perpetuated her internal myths.

The other group members' responses to the therapist's decision to ban Laurie from the group were twofold. On one level, they felt and expressed relief, and were in agreement that Laurie was out of place with the group's goals. On another level, they were discomfited by the therapist's swift intervention and use of power to relieve the group of Laurie's influence. The implied consensus was that Laurie was troubled and needed psychotherapy more than they did.

Under ideal circumstances, the psychotherapeutic solution would have been to help Laurie become aware of how her antagonistic stance was abrasive and contributed to her becoming an outcast. The group could have rallied and supported her recovery. Having the transference from her past be exposed within the group experience was fertile ground for significant work and potential healing. Unfortunately the concept of "timing" was of the essence. "Timing" makes perfect sense to a psychotherapist but feels vague to most patients. By and large, patients do not conceptualize that the right "timing" is crucial for therapeutic resolutions to occur.

The failure not to be able to help Laurie left a realistic mark on the group's consciousness. Not everyone can be helped at the time when help is available. Everyone has a specific pace and "timing" for their understandings and self-realizations.

The major players in this episode were Laurie, Mona, Bonnie, and the therapist. The other members assumed the role of follower. Patty, the kindergarten teacher, came close to being the joker of the group. She had a vivacious presence and lively outlook that brought humor and good cheer to the group's process.

Most groups develop their own particular character. Each member adds to the group's richness and flavor, bringing with them the inevitable twists and turns that exist in life.

CRCRCR

CHALLENGING PATIENTS

Patients can be problematic and challenging for the psychotherapist for a variety of reasons. It is impossible to encounter no challenges in the therapeutic relationships, or to see oneself as such a capable therapist that any challenge can be handled and resolved. It is important to keep in mind that psychotherapists are not supposed to be all-knowing. Like everyone else, psychotherapists are humans with flaws, fallibilities, and limitations. Recognizing these limitations and being able to communicate them in a therapeutic and insightful manner are essential in order to be effective with the work. Hiding the limitations usually backfires and discredits the therapist. There are times when the therapist's limitations are not conducive to effective counseling, so a patient has to be referred elsewhere. In order to make an appropriate referral, the therapist has to be not invested in their ego to be able to let go of the relationship.

Challenging issues may arise without hindering the therapeutic outcomes. However, any challenge, major or minor, can become problematic if the therapist is unaware and/or resistant to growth and self-development.

Some examples of the challenges that contain growth potential for both therapist and patient are as follows.

Challenging Patients

When the therapist and the client have opposite genders, the male/female sexual dynamic becomes a component in the therapeutic relationship. Homosexually inclined therapists and clients can also experience similar dynamics and challenges.

It is inevitable that male patients will attempt at some point to make a play at seducing their female therapist (or same sex therapist, if homosexual), if they find them attractive. This is usually a test of the therapist's strength and fallibilities. If the therapist can be seduced, they are rendered powerless and ineffective as a mentor. The therapist's awareness can rescue this attempt from disaster. The therapist needs to seize this opportunity to clarify the confines of the therapeutic relationship and define its boundaries as a way of providing safety and trust. When the male patient realizes that a seduction is unlikely, feelings of trust, and the ability to reveal and work more productively, increase.

Sometimes the male patient relates as a child looking for a mother or father, and projects the transference on to a mature, female or male therapist. This transference can be important information that will expound upon the son's expectations of a mother or father. But if the mature female or male therapist is also looking for a son in their patient, then the exchange becomes murky and complex, and the therapeutic goals confused.

The same can happen in reverse. A female patient can attempt to seduce her male or female therapist. Again, this attempt is to check for safety, and to test the therapist's strength and ability to be effective. If he or she can be conquered, then he or she is not considered worthy.

The female patient can also transfer the father-wound or mother-wound on to a male or female therapist. Sometimes the female patient is looking for a father or mother figure, but the therapist misunderstands and responds as a man or woman aroused by a helpless young woman. The results of such counter-transferences are experienced as traumatic and fraught with betrayal by the female patient. The therapist's awareness and understanding of these potential traps are paramount for therapeutic success. If the traps can be thwarted and used insightfully, the therapeutic outcomes can be considerable. Safety, trust, and credibility can then be restored.

Therapeutic parameters and boundaries must be considered sacred by both therapist and patient. The space where therapy is conducted needs to be described to the patient as a place of safety. The patient must be able to feel free to reveal and express their innermost self, while the therapist should provide safe harbor and become the anchor for the patient to hold on to.

Most problems and difficulties arise when these set parameters are somehow breached. Since psychotherapists are also human and vulnerable, they can compromise the therapeutic boundaries by getting over-attached to their patients. The degree of attachment can run from over-curiosity and interference in the patient's life, to falling in love and becoming sexually attracted to the patient. Unless the therapist's awareness intervenes and creates the appropriate recovery and perspective, the patient has to be referred to someone else when the therapeutic objectives and therapist's objectivity have been compromised. The ability to see and sense the patient with clarity and without need and prejudice are no longer operational.

Other challenging encounters arise when the patient is more intellectually adept than their therapist. In this case, the patient has the ability to outsmart the therapist's strategies and interventions, and build strong defenses. The credibility of the therapist comes into question. By turn, the therapist's defensive responses can further dissolve or hinder the therapeutic relationship. It is significant to note that psychological wellbeing and positive mental health have nothing to do with intelligence. All human emotions are primitive in nature, and therefore equalize the human playing field. The dance around "who is the smartest" is a power game.

The best strategy is to be open and upfront with one's personal limitations.

There are times when the psychotherapist feels dislike and becomes judgmental when reacting to a patient. Acute, strong responses usually indicate counter-transferences that stem from unresolved issues in the therapist's own psychology. If the clues to the dislike and judgments can be deciphered and understood in the context of the therapeutic relationship, there is potential for growth and meaning for both patient and therapist. If the work to ascertain this information is more arduous and complex, invading the time allotted to the patient, then the therapist should refer the client to some other facility.

A similar process can be applied when the therapist experiences boredom and restlessness in a patient's presence. This lack of interest in the patient can be indicative of the therapist's personal blocks and issues. It may also provide valid information for detecting the dynamics of the patient's boring behavior in others relationships. If what is gleaned can be applied constructively to the work in progress, and then positive therapeutic outcomes can emerge. However, if the boredom is overwhelming, referral is in order.

Sometimes the psychotherapist can be offended or irritated by the patient's body odors and/or idiosyncratic habits. The body odors can be strong perspiration, dirt, or bad breath. As a result, it is difficult for them to focus and be fully present.

Certain ticks, nail biting, nose picking, burping, and farting can also distract a therapist's concentration and full attention. It takes great courage and delicacy to express these discomforts to a patient and to ask if anything can be done to change these things. Most people are reluctant to comment and give feedback on someone's physical annoyances.

For example, patients may not be aware that their odor is offensive and may be leading others to avoid their company. They may have assumed erroneously that that there were other reasons for people's avoiding them. Therefore it has therapeutic significance to explore a patient's self-awareness in this regard. Sometimes, simple solutions can alleviate huge misconceptions, and change the course of life's direction.

Depending on the psychotherapist's practice, there will be times when a patient is forced to attend therapy due to their involvement with the legal system. Therapy may be court appointed or required as psychological support to an ongoing legal dispute. Most of these patients are reluctant to participate in therapy, so their performances are perfunctory and/or manipulative. They resist and express ill will toward the psychotherapist's attempts at therapeutic undertakings. If an inspiring event or thought does not emerge which transcends the legal requirement for attendance, then time spent in therapy will likely be tedious and wasteful.

People who are forced into therapy by the legal systems can, at times, be criminals with anti-social and/or violent behavior. The psychotherapist's legitimate reaction to these characters may be fear, but this can be a deterrent to achieving positive progress in therapy. Fear objectifies, demonizes and diminishes the humanity of a person. The labels and diagnoses attached to an individual as a result of deeds preformed do not necessarily define the whole person. If the psychotherapist cannot overcome their fear, then therapeutic attempts are bound to fall short.

Besides fear, the psychotherapist's moral indignation and personal values may prevent them from encountering a patient on objective levels. Pedophiles, pimps, prostitutes, and people who have committed rape, abuse, and murder are examples of the kind of people who might arouse strong moral judgments that can take precedence over the therapist's ability to be objective. There are times when fear is valid, psychotherapy does not have priority, and the call to law enforcement is necessary.

Psychopaths, sociopaths and borderline patients have been known to run circles around psychotherapists. They are artful manipulators who have no compunction against distorting communication exchanges for their own benefit and gain.

The major difficulty in dealing with a psychopath or sociopath is that there are no accepted rules or understandings for "proper" conduct. For the psychopath, anything goes for them to gain the upper hand in an exchange. Laws, morality, civil conduct, caring, empathy for the other, and honesty have little meaning and/or are non-existent for the psychopath and sociopath. It is very difficult to reach or touch the humanity of such people. To administer therapy requires a psychotherapist who is highly skilled and knowledgeable in this area.

In general, people who are forced into therapy are not candidates for acquiring the maximum benefits from the process. Older children and teens that have been given no choice but to be in therapy by their families and/or schools can also be challenging for therapeutic work. However, there can be opportunities to inspire and motivate reluctant patients to make better use of their enforced time. Offering to show them how to learn about and develop a deeper understanding of the self, unexpected aspects of their personality and behaviors can stimulate the interest and inspire participation of those who do not choose psychotherapy on their own.

Paranoid patients are another group of people who are challenging to work with. The acute sensitivities and mistrusts that they experience prevent or make difficult the establishment of a relationship. Patience and highly tuned skills are required to make connections and to offer the possibility of conducting any kind of therapy. If trust can be established, it will always be on thin ice that can crack at any hint of miscommunication. Therefore, the therapeutic process is delicate, slow, and tenuous at every step.

There are also patients who have strongholds for their defenses and guard them with arsenals. Any attempts to approach the defenses results in attacks of rage, anger, ridicule, dark humor, flight, or silence. Winning their trust can be a lengthy process. Care and creativity, the appropriate design, strategy, and individualized steps are the required implementations.

When patients do not pay their fee or dodge this aspect of the relationship, the therapist, willing or not, becomes personally affected by the dynamic, and is forced to confront the issue. Novice therapists are usually uncomfortable with asking for payments for counseling sessions. More seasoned therapists are comfortable with the monetary exchanges and might even feel insulted or not valued if a patient shirks making any payments due.

The exchange of payment often adds a realistic dimension to the therapeutic relationship; it is reflective and revealing of both the patient's and the therapist's expectations. It is best to have established the ground rules for payments before the onset of the therapeutic process. In this respect, the upfront attitude communicated by the therapist will allow the patient to make their decision prior to any investments in the venture and reduce potential misunderstandings.

There are occasions when the patient and therapist experience similar life events, simultaneously. Loss of someone close, a terminal illness, a divorce, or a betrayal is some examples of such possible simultaneous occurrences. There can be advantages and disadvantages for the work in progress as both therapist and client react to these similar occurrences. If the therapist is too close to the situation and unable to establish the distance necessary to see the larger picture, the therapeutic work is at risk. If the therapist can convey empathy and understanding derived from the situation, and can also maintain objectivity so as to note wherever the client has blind spots, then the therapy can be very potent.

If the patient's life experiences trigger psychological issues that reveal where the therapist might be blocked or stuck in development, the ability to conduct effective psychotherapy for the patient is compromised. The therapist has to be competent to explore the psychological dynamics of areas where they have some knowledge and experience. The artful therapist can also imagine and empathize with life situations in which they have had no experience. However, blocked psychological issues will handicap the therapist from thorough investigations. It can also stimulate fear in the therapist when their defenses are triggered while working with a patient. It is best for the therapist to acknowledge to him or her any areas that are unresolved, and then to seek supervision and appropriate guidance.

ଔଔଔଔ

The following case presentations provide brief glimpses of patients that have been challenging.

Case Study: Amanda

Amanda was hospitalized for attempting to commit suicide. This episode was her third attempt in five years. She was under observation at the hospital with a seventy-two-hour hold.

She was in her late thirties, very attractive and educated, and displayed a flamboyant, superior air. There was a disconnection between her behavior and her surroundings. It is as if she was a guest at a resort rather than a patient in a hospital psychiatric ward under strict observation. She was charming to the nurses and staff but expected quality service. Her psychiatrist referred her for outpatient psychotherapy after her release. Her diagnosis on record was Borderline Disorder with Sociopathic Tendencies. This diagnosis did not bode well for private practice.

From the onset, Amanda provided excuses and profuse apologies for not being able to make her payments for therapy sessions. She was always without cash, checkbook, or credit card, and she would forget to mail in her payment. She appeared at the therapist's office on a daily basis, regardless of her set appointments. She was always in crisis and in need of immediate assistance. Amanda left numerous notes stained with blood spots and strange needy phone messages that caused concern and worry if not attended to.

In consulting with her psychiatrist, it became obvious that he had basically washed his hands of this case and referred her in order to get rid of "the headache."

Amanda was relentless in her ability to create crisis and chaos. Apparently, she had a long history of relationships with mental health professionals whom she had rendered ineffective, and then never paid their fees. Amanda had become a master of inventing scenes to seduce people into coming to her aid. She enjoyed the victory of her seductions and milked her victims until they were dry and powerless. She personified the classic Spider Woman. She excelled at this vampire syndrome, and her target group was mental health professionals.

The relationship with the current therapist came to an abrupt halt after an episode in which the police had to be notified. Amanda had left long knives and a blood-splattered note on the therapist's doorstep along with the threat of yet another suicide. When the therapist called in the law, Amanda became enraged. She fired the therapist, skipped town, and disappeared into the sunset. She owed the naïve therapist over ten thousand dollars in unpaid bills.

Case Study: Jack

Jack the pimp was a court-appointed case. He was required to be in therapy for twelve sessions. It was obvious from his demeanor that he was just adhering to the system's regulations and had no intention of making personal use of the ruling to undergo therapy.

Jack had the stereotypical appearance of a pimp. He wore a brightly-colored silk shirt open to the belly, tight jeans, gold chains around his neck, and gold loops in his ears. He had shoulder length brown hair tied back in a ponytail. His heritage seemed to be Slavic.

While in evasive, meaningless conversation, his nonverbal communication sent a different message. He sat loosely with his legs spread widely apart, casually stroking his genitals and closely watching the female therapist's reaction. His tactics were designed to test the power dynamic between himself and the therapist using a manner both familiar and typical to him. He was measuring the therapist's strength and looking for ways to permeate the parameters of his enforced sentence. He was throwing out a challenge and not very invested in the outcome. He seemed to be playing around or entertaining himself.

Confronting the exchange head-on was the best course of action by the therapist. Ignoring the challenge could have communicated fear and undermined the therapist's ability to be effective. Confrontation would have impact if the therapist could convey that she understood the intention behind the gestures and was not intimidated.

Intimidation and provoking fear in order to take over the control were skills that Jack had developed expertly in his work as a pimp. It was natural for him to try the same maneuvers with any woman who had control over his time and situation.

Confronting Jack's need to intimidate and inspire fear, then overpower and take control of any situation that he was obligated to participate in were the first entrées into creating a scenario where an actual therapeutic encounter was possible.

Jack did not back down easily. He continued to attempt intimidation at every turn. If the therapist could pass the tests and reach beyond the power tactics to touch Jack's vulnerabilities, however, the therapeutic aims had a chance to flourish.

ଓଓଓଓ

Case Study: Allen and Nora

Allen and Nora came for therapy as a couple. They also brought their infant daughter and three-year-old son with them. It was difficult to ascertain and clarify their reasons for wanting therapy.

They lived outside of the city on five acres of land, which they were cultivating to grow fruits and vegetables. They looked more like brother and sister rather than husband and wife. Both were wispy looking, blonde, and disheveled.

Challenging Patients

The children were exceptionally quiet. The boy was very shy and hid behind his mother. Allen had a strong, booming voice, incongruent with his frail body. Nora spoke softly, almost in a whisper. Her eyes were huge and glistened with tears. She mostly watched her husband and echoed whatever he said.

Allen's conversation was disjointed and made little sense. He spoke of gods and goddesses and evil spirits. He expounded on his God-given rights as a father to initiate his children into the rituals of the "harvest" and the blessings of mother earth. He claimed that he had already initiated his son for the harvest of life. He wanted to initiate his daughter while she was still an infant, but his wife, Nora, had opposed him. Nora claimed that their daughter was much too young. She had caught Allen on the verge of the initiation and stopped the process. Allen had been so angry that he had shoved her against the wall, hurting her head. They wanted an outside opinion from a therapist in order to resolve their dispute and to receive advice on the correct age for the initiation to take place.

When asked what exactly the initiation entailed, they described a bizarre ceremony that involved fruit offerings to the gods and goddesses, charms to ward off evil, candles, music, and singing. The act performed by Allen to complete the initiation was to disrobe the child and suck his or her genitals until the "juices of life flowed."

Both Allen and Nora spoke earnestly and matter-of-factly, as though this ceremony was a righteous, normal ritual performed by everyone. Their dispute was regarding the appropriate age for a child to experience the ceremony. Apparently, their son had been initiated on his birthday at the age of one and every birthday since. Allen wanted to perform the "rites" on their three-month-old daughter and Nora wanted to wait until she was also one year old, like her brother. The notion of child abuse had not penetrated their consciousness.

It was relevant to conclude that Allen and Nora were operating in some kind of psychotic collusion with each other. Any reasonable psychotherapeutic intervention administered from a private practice seemed out of the question at that point. In fact, therapeutic intervention for the couple was deemed to be secondary. The children's safety and finding them a sanctuary was the first priority.

According to the dictates of law, Child Protective Services had to be notified. The tragic consequence of separating children from their parents was inevitable for this case. Allen and Nora had no awareness of their wrongdoings, and were outraged by the separation, feeling betrayed by the therapist. Allen had already displayed some violence by pushing Nora against the wall. However, rescuing the children was critical. Helping to find a therapeutic facility for the parents could follow.

ଈଈଈ

These three cases portray difficult encounters with patients during the course of therapy. The therapist's skills and expertise were challenged in the attempts to discover the appropriate means for intervention and therapy. Challenges will arise throughout the professional lifespan of all therapists. Usually, experience and a continually open mind teaches the psychotherapist how to gain the confidence and sharpen the skills necessary to find solutions that will be helpful in any situations that present themselves for therapy.

ଏଠାଠା

INNOVATIVE INTERVENTIONS

Psychotherapy is conducted primarily within the safe parameters of an office and through the method of verbal communications. However, interventions can also be constructed spontaneously and creatively to suit a patient's immediate needs and struggles. It is useful to have some knowledge of the alternative psychotherapeutic tools that are available and been shown to be effective. It is important to utilize these resources as suggested outlines and to tailor them to the individualize tasks at hand. Choosing the appropriate timing for an innovative intervention is an artful practice. It is a judgment call, and depends on the psychotherapist's ability to be versatile, confident, and comfortable with spontaneity.

Innovative interventions work best when the moment calls for a change of direction in order to unblock and/or refresh the dynamics and flow of therapy. When patients experience stagnation in their awareness, understanding, and realizations, then innovative measures can help to unblock the process and bring forth fresh views. Creative tools can also open the pathways between unconscious thoughts and images, and bring them into conscious awareness.

For the most part, patients dwell in the known territories of their psychological terrain. They always display some resistance when the known boundaries are pressed to expand, and they are urged to venture into what is unknown and yet to be discovered. Talk therapies are most effective in sorting out perceptions, clarifying feelings, reorganizing understandings, and reinterpreting the significance of information and events. The aim of experiential therapies is to create occurrences to which the patient has not stored any previous reactions. An unexpected incident usually dislodges old interpretations and allows the patient to have immediate and new reactions. Responses and inputs are played out live in the presence of the therapist. Exploring new territory is very therapeutic and powerful if the patient is open and willing. Expanding the patient's awareness and repertoire is the goal of most therapeutic endeavors.

It will be difficult to describe all the experiences that can be devised in the moment to help a patient to transition to deeper levels of awareness. However, there are certain experiential interventions that seem to provide a shorter and more succinct means to therapeutic outcomes. A short summary of these methods is discussed below.

The states of the mind and its emotions usually have an impact on the body. Breathing, posture, and the ways in which the body is held and carried describe a patient's emotional state more explicitly than verbal reports. Guiding the patient through breathing exercises and using relaxation techniques can alleviate some of the anxiety and frustration experienced in certain moments. Intense emotions often prevent deep work and fog the mind from clarity.

Sometimes just discussing anger and pain isn't sufficient for the patient to get to the heart of the problem. Tearing old phone books, pounding into a cushion, and/or kicking a soft object can provide the opportunity to experience the emotion intensely and then find an avenue of release. Expressions of emotion are usually the outer layers of any issues to be worked on. Once the outer layers are stripped away, the core has a chance to be revealed.

If a patient or couple is in a power struggle, arm wrestling is a vehicle that can permit an "acting out" of the dynamic that characterizes their struggle. The results can stimulate discussion and explorations of the precipitating issues involved.

Deep relaxation exercises can at times lead a patient to enter an area that has been buried and closely defended in the mind. In relaxing the body, the forbidden area can be revisited and released in order for healing to take place.

Imagery and the uses of metaphors often communicate meanings more succinctly and completely than mere explanations and narratives. Like poetry, images reflect pictures from the unconscious mind that cut through the defenses in one's conscious awareness. Metaphors also create images that can communicate profound descriptions and depict struggles in a few short strokes.

Free dancing, movement, and changes in posture are other methods for releasing tension and pent-up energies. In changing the expressions and rhythms of the body, the mind also opens and shakes loose from blocks and defenses that are in place.

Music is often a direct route for bringing emotions and sentiments to the forefront. Music is a universal source of stimulation and enhancement for the imagination. Specific instruments seem to evoke specific emotions.

Using mediums from arts and crafts like clay, paint, crayons, and/or simple drawings can be another means for the unconscious to communicate the feelings and emotions that are felt in the moment. The interpretation of art therapy, however, requires special skill and study.

Role-play is a useful tool for patients who are having conflicts with family members and in other relationships. It is a prolific method for injecting understanding. The patient assumes the role of the person who is the object of conflict and then imagines his or her dynamic with the issues in question and interacts from their points of view. Psychodrama works similar to role-play but is for group and family therapies. It involves assuming the roles of others and interacting from their perspectives. Both role-play and psychodrama are effective tools for resolving inter and intra-conflicts, as well as enhancing empathy and understanding for others.

At times the use of video and photographs can be a direct and effective transmission of feedback. Some patients do not have a sense of their body image or how they project their personalities, nor of its impact on others. Photographs and video are a means to demonstrate some of these aspects of the self in concrete forms. Before and after pictures or videos describe events and changes that can occur during the course of therapy, and can also lend substantive support to the process.

There are many other experiential methods of therapies. However, most require special training and competence to implement. Bioenergetics and/or other body-orientated therapies, hypnotherapy, dream work, dance and art therapies, Watsu (water therapy), and nature walks are some of the many interesting and useful experiential methods that need further training and certification.

ೲೲ

Case Study: Grant and Reyna

The following case study describes some uses and misuses of experiential interventions.

Grant and Reyna were both successful physicians in their mid-forties; they had two children. They were articulate and intelligent individuals who related to each other through somewhat sarcastic banter. Their decision to come for psychotherapy was due primarily to their concern for their children. Both admitted to being unable to stop fighting incessantly and without much control. They were also fighting in front of the children and worried about the impact it might leave on them. Their main goal for therapy was to develop some control and cease the fighting.

Exploring the dynamic of their discourse, it became apparent that the fights were triggered by minutia and conducted in strong verbal exchanges characterized by wit, sarcasm, judgment, criticism, and ridicule. They could not pinpoint the source of their unhappiness with each other. They mostly complained about each other's behaviors. Grant preferred that Reyna be a stay-at-home mom. Reyna felt that her education, training, and expertise would be wasted if she stayed home. Reyna was annoyed with Grant for allowing the family dog to follow him everywhere. She wanted the dog to stay out of the bedrooms. They carried on expressing discomforts and grievances, but both admitted that all the differences could be worked out if they could stop picking on each other. They did not understand their compulsion to belittle and hurt one another without being able to exercise restraint or control.

An interesting factor to note was that Grant and Reyna refrained from looking directly at each other. Their communication was through talk and their eyes went everywhere except on each other.

It came as a revelation when it was suggested that the verbal abuse between them was a defense used so as not to be close and loving; also, there might be deep hurt and anger buried in their relationship. They conceded that it was possible that they had suffered from some hurt. However, they could not imagine what the content of that hurt might be. They quickly reverted back to sarcasm and putdowns that held a measure of entertainment for them, as well strong defense/offense tactics.

It was obvious that Grant and Reyna were well versed in the art of verbal battling. The situation seemed ripe for other types of interventions. Role-play was attempted. They were asked to switch roles and imagine themselves in the other person's shoes, then to talk to one another from that perspective. It soon became clear that role-play was not the appropriate technique for them to generate empathy and understanding. Their personalities and psychological dynamics were so similar and their defense/offense strategies so finely tuned to one another that switching roles hardly made a difference. This technique merely revealed a continuation of the same type of non-stop verbal abuse. The power struggle that played on the intellectual and verbal levels between them was so evenly matched that no headway was made with this technique.

Arm wrestling was attempted next. Neither Reyna nor Grant could take arm wrestling seriously. They played at it. Since Grant was obviously stronger and could easily beat Reyna, he made a joke of it. They mostly tickled and lightly pinched each other. The horsing about injected laughter and ease into the dynamic, taking their minds off the bickering. But the arm wrestling did not expound on the power struggles between them; instead, the suggestion of the game broke the ice, ushering in more ease and camaraderie.

Next, they were asked to sit across from each other, make eye contact, and sit close but not touch or talk. The assignment was to just look at each other and see what happened.

They were very uncomfortable with this exercise. They joked and made faces at each other. It took a while before they could settle down and actually make eye contact. When the connection was made, a serious quiet came about. They looked at each other for at least ten minutes, and then their faces changed to reveal pain, regret, and sorrow. Slowly more feelings emerged. Grant's eyes first clouded with tears that began to flow down his cheeks. Reyna too began to cry and heave. They just cried, looking at each other for another five minutes. Then, spontaneously, they fell into each other's arms and cried even harder, holding one another. Clearly a breakthrough had taken place.

The discussion that followed revealed a misunderstanding from the onset of their marriage. Both had assumed their marriage had been out of convenience and practicality, not based on love.

Reyna had been engaged to marry another man whom she had loved deeply. He died in an auto accident before they could marry. Grant had also been in love with a woman who abandoned him to marry his brother. Grant and Reyna met when they were on the rebound. Reyna got pregnant with their first child and they married with resignation and complacency, not deep love. They had grown to care and respect one another, but were afraid to allow themselves to get too close or let their guards down. Both had experienced loss, hurt, and betrayal from people whom they had trusted and who they thought of as the love of their lives. They did not want to risk the pain of disappointment and loss all over again. They liked each other. They had discovered that they had a lot in common. They adored their children and were proud of the life they had built together. At present, their feelings for their past loves were dim and just painful memories. Reyna and Grant's marriage, under the surface, had the characteristics of a healthy and loving union.

ରୋରୋରୋ

Psychological dynamics

The significant clue displayed during the verbal abuse that occurred between Reyna and Grant was the deliberate avoidance of eye contact. They never looked at each other directly. Despite all the banter and noise, they did not talk to each other. They made no intimate connections; they talked at each other. It was like watching them throwing fireballs in the other's direction. The intent of all their communications was to safeguard their hearts, not to be vulnerable and get too close.

The enforced eye contact exercise provided Grant and Reyna the opportunity to cut through the verbal, abusive defense mechanisms and be able to connect with authentic emotion and feeling. They could no longer use each other as an object that represented their fears from the past. They were brought into the immediate present and a connection was able to occur on a subjective, personal and unavoidable level.

To the outside observer, it was apparent from the start that these two people cared for each other. However, both fought hard against their softer feelings and perpetuated the battle lines in order to safeguard against the closeness that had been growing between them without their volition. These two people had the potential to be excellent marriage partners. They had a great deal of positive characteristics in common. Even the wit, sarcasm, and ridicule they expressed had a certain connected rhythm and operated as if in sync.

The compulsion to fight was a defense mechanism for self-protection. The harder they fought, the more likely that they were feeling vulnerable. In some part of their psyche, there was an awareness of the fondness and caring that had grown during their marriage and the births of their children. They had created a family and a life together. They were equally successful and had respect for the other's accomplishments. They were also devoted to their children.

Reyna and Grant had suffered trauma and loss from their previous relationships. Their reactions to these losses had been devastating for both of them. They came together on the rebound, with neither of them having recovered nor cognizant of the trauma they had experienced. They began their lives together carrying symptoms of posttraumatic stress syndrome. Even trying to imagine being together with a free and open expression of their caring, brought up painful anxiety for both of them. Any notions of expressing love and closeness were fraught with convoluted emotions and forbidden signposts that emanated from past traumas of loss and pain.

Exploring how much Reyna and Grant had in common was the therapeutic strategy that helped them to acknowledge that they were on the same side rather than always in opposition. Reinforcing their bond as a team was significant. They were habituated to operating as solo players. Their common behaviors extended to similar reactions to fear and loss, and a need to self-protect even at the expense of hurting their partner.

The eye exercise was cathartic for both Reyna and Grant. It enabled an opening of the floodgates for pain that had been buried from their past but had ongoing control of their behaviors in the relationship. The tears that flowed were a means of letting go, and washed out the past hurts so that a fresh beginning became possible.

The task of psychotherapy was to help Grant and Reyna disconnect from the controls of their past hurts and bring them into the present so that they could respond and be more fully available in the immediate moment. The baggage from their past had been ruling their psychology and contaminated their views. The past was an ever-present obstacle. It had prevented them from forming a relationship that operated as a balanced duet. In fact, the ghosts of their past loves disrupted their duet and became a quartet instead. Reyna and Grant could not see each other as individuals. They were two people living with two other ghosts. They were not able to appreciate one another's attributes, nor the successful marriage partnership that they had built. They saw their relationship through the veil of betrayal, loss, and abandonment.

Reyna and Grant had not said goodbye to the partners they had loved, cherished, and eventually lost. A therapeutic ceremony devised for letting go and formally saying goodbye gave them an opportunity to disconnect from the traumas they had sustained. They were asked to write letters to their past lovers. The content of the letters included their feelings and the pain they had suffered. The letters ended with declarations of farewell. They were asked to also find a photograph of their past lover, and bring the letters and pictures to the therapy session. With ceremony and ritual, the letters and pictures were placed together and set on fire. Since no resistance ensued from this proposal, the ritual provided a formal ending that had been long overdue.

Reyna and Grant came to realize and value their personal strengths, as well as the strengths in their marriage. Their compulsion to fight and remain unattached no longer made sense or was viable. The fighting had served a psychological purpose that no longer existed. Recovery and positive prognosis was high for this couple.

CRCRCR

CONCLUSION

The concluding remarks are primarily addressed to students of psychology who are contemplating becoming psychotherapists or who are already in training for the field.

One of the most fulfilling experiences in life is the moment of deep contact with another being. In the therapeutic space, these moments of deep contact are likely to emerge much more frequently than in most walks of life.

The therapeutic space contains a built-in invitation for authenticity. This permission is conducive to allowing the discard of defensive armors that exist in daily encounters.

The safety that is created in the therapeutic space is sacred. Psychotherapists are privileged and honor-bound to cherish and protect this dictate.

The paths for healing demand honesty and authenticity.

The psychotherapist becomes the guardian of the therapeutic space and is committed to its preservation. Only then can the possibilities to revitalize the wounded soul and rejuvenate the tired spirit occur.

It is most liberating and satisfying to be allowed to be fully present in the moment and available to another being. The

Conclusion

authentic presence is a necessary condition in order to be able to guide and discover the paths for healing and wellbeing.

Creativity, a willingness to be adventurous, caring, resourcefulness, acute awareness, and alert attentiveness are the optimum states of enlivenment for positive mental and physical health.

"We must be willing to let go of the life we planned so as to have the life that is waiting for us."
—Joseph Campbell

ର୍ଥର୍ଥର୍ଥ

ACKNOWLEDGMENTS

I have had numerous wonderful teachers who have given me energy and wisdom in the pursuit of becoming a psychotherapist. Dr. Stan Charnofsky was my first and foremost teacher and mentor whose influence I still carry. I was fortunate to have him introduce me to the field of psychotherapy and Humanistic Psychology, forty years ago, at a Master's program at Cal State Northridge.

My nephews Ashgan and Jahan Djalali ignited the inspiration to write this book. Their curiosity and interests in my work were the impetus to sketch and elaborate on a frame that finally translated in to developing this project.

My siblings H. F. Djalali and Parnian Kummer have held an encouraging light on this endeavor and kept it shining. Their support and care has enabled me to forge ahead.

My mother's lovely spirit is ever present in my heart. Her belief and confidence in me has given sustenance and strength in whatever venture I undertake.

I thank Dr. Robert Rosenstone for his considerable wise advice. Also, he introduced me to my wonderful editor, Ms. Kathryn Galán. Kathryn's swift responses, her abilities and knowledge of the language, her care and conscientious work have been undeniable, most valuable, and much appreciated.

Acknowledgments

I thank Ms. Carol Thompson who proofread the manuscript. Kathryn described Carol's contribution as "most elegant" and I concur. Don at Webmark arranged the graphics. His patience and versatility is duly noted. My good friend, Ms. Nahid Massoud, is the photo artist. How she managed to coax me into cooperating for a pose is indicative of her many powers

Last but not least, I am grateful to the patients and students I have had the privilege to be of significance. They have been the most profound teachers in understanding human behavior.

త్రత్రత్రత్రత్ర

Veis Djalali

ରେରେରେରେରେ

ABOUT THE AUTHOR

Veis Djalali has a doctorate from the University of Southern California and is in private practice in Santa Monica, California. She has been in the field of psychotherapy since the mid-1970s, and has accumulated a vast variety of experiences. She has been a professor at Cal State Dominguez Hills, Antioch University, and UCLA Extension. She has also worked in hospitals, mental health and drug abuse clinics, and with a training psychotherapist.

ⱭⱭⱭ

REFERENCES

So many works of major notables have influenced the thought formulations that have been processed to produce this book. It would be impossible to cite them all. Only a significant fraction was chosen below to exemplify the flavor, orientation, and framework, and to suggest additional reading and resources. The list can easily be extended into volumes!

Becker, Ernest. *The Denial Of Death* (2nd edition). New York: Free Press, 1997.

Bentall, Richard P. *Madness Explained: Psychosis And Human Nature.* New York: Penguin, 2004.

Berger, Kathleen S. *The Developing Person Through the Life Span.* (8th edition). New York: Worth Publishers, 2011.

Bergantino, Len. *Psychotherapy, Insight, and Style: The Existential Moment.* Northvale, New Jersey: Janson Aronson Inc., 1986.

Berne, Eric. *Games People Play: The Psychology of Human Relations.* New York: Grove Press, 1964 (1978 Reprint).

Bly, Robert & Woodman, Marion. *The Maiden King.* New York: Henry Holt & Co., 1998.

References

Bradshaw, John. *Homecoming: Reclaiming and Championing Your Inner Child*. New York: Bantam Books, 1992.

Bradshaw, John. *Family Secrets*. New York: Bantam Books, 1995.

Brown, Nina W. *Psychoeducational Groups: Process And Practice*. New York: Brunner-Routledge, 2004.

Bugental, James F. *Psychotherapy and Process*. New York: McGraw-Hill College, 1978.

Bugental, James F. *The Search for Existential Identity: Patient-Therapist Dialogues in Humanistic Psychotherapy*. New York: Jossey-Bass, 1976.

Bugental, James F. *The Search For Authenticity*. New York: Holt, Rinehart & Winston Inc., 1965.

Bugental, James F. *The Art Of The Psychotherapist: How to Develop the Skills That Take Psychotherapy Beyond Science*. New York: W.W. Norton & Co., 1992.

Bugenthal, James E *Psychotherapy Isn't What You Think*. Arizona: Zeig, Tucker, & Theisen, 1999.

Calhoun, Lawrence G. & Tedeschi, Richard G. *Handbook of Posttraumatic Growth: Research and Practice*. Mahwah, New Jersey: Erlbaum, 2006.

Camus, Albert. *The Myth of Sisyphus*. "The Absurd Man: Don Juanism." Vintage: Reissue Edition, 1991.

Carkhuff, Robert R. & Berenson, Bernard. G. *Beyond Counseling and Therapy*. New York: Holt, Rinehart & Winston, Inc., 1964.

Carkhuff, Robert R. *Helping and Human Relations: A Primer for Lay and Professional Helpers*. New York: Holt, Rinehart & Winston Inc., 1969.

Cash, Thomas F. & Pruzinsky, Thomas. editors. *Body Images, Developmental Deviance and Change*. New York: Guilford Press, 1990.

Connidls, Ingrid A. *Family Ties And Aging*. (2nd edition) California: Sage Publications, 2009.

Derlega, Valerian T., Hendrick, Susan S., Winstead, B.A. & Berg, John H. *Psychotherapy as a Personal Relationship*. New York: Guilford Press, 1991.

Erickson, Milton H. & Rossi, Ernest L. Hypnotherapy: An Exploratory Casebook. New York: Irvington Publishers, Inc., 1979.

Feder, Bud & Frew, Jon. Editors. *Beyond the Hot Seat Revisited: Gestalt Approaches to Group*. California: Los Angeles Gestalt Institute Press, 2008.

Fox, John. "Eating Disorders And Emotions." Clinical Psychology and Psychotherapy: 16, July 2009. 237-239.

Frankal, Victor E. *Man's Search for Meaning: An Introduction to Logotherapy*. New York: Washington Square Press, 1963.

Franz, Marie-Louise Von. *Shadow and Evil in Fairytales: Animus and Anima In Fairytales*. Switzerland; Spring Publications, 1974.

Frisch, Maria J. Franko, Debra L. & Herzog, David. *Arts-based Therapies In Treatment of Eating Disorders*. 14(2), 2006. 131-42.

References

Fromm, Erich. *Escape From Freedom*. New York: Avon Books, 1941.

Fromm, Erich. *The Art of Loving*. New York: Harper & Row Inc., 1956.

Fromm, Erich. *The Art of Being*. New York: The Continuum Publishing Co., 1992.

Freud, Sigmund. *Sexuality and The Psychology Of Love*. New York: Simon & Schuster, 1963.

Gerstein, Larry H. & Heppner, P.P., editors. *International Handbook Of Cross-Cultural Counseling: Cultural Assumptions and Practices Worldwide*. California: Sage Publications, 2009.

Gurman, Allen S. *Casebook of Marital Therapy*. New York: Guilford Press, 1985.

Hall, Guy. & Hivernel, Francoise. *Theory and Practice In Child Psychoanalysis: An Introduction To Francoise Dolto's Work*. Karnac Books, 2009.

Haley, Jay. *Uncommon Therapy: The Psychiatric Techniques of Milton Erickson*. New York: W.W. Norton & Co. Inc., 1973.

Harrod, Wendy J., Welch, Bridget K. & Kushkowski, Jeffry. Thirty-One Years Of Group Research in Social Psychology Quarterly (1975-2005)." *Current Research In Social Psychology*, 14, 2009. 75-103.

Hartmann, Uwe. "Sigmund Freud and His Impact On Our Understanding Of Male Sexual Dysfunction". *The Journal of Sexual Medicine*. 6 (8): 2009. 2332-2339.

Henderson, Nan. *Resiliency in Action: Practical Ideas For Overcoming Risks And Building Strengths In Youth, Families And Communities.* 2nd ed. Ojai, California: Resiliency In Action Publishers, 2007.

Hendricks, Marion N. "Focusing-Orientated/ Experiential Psychotherapy." www.Focusing.org. 2001.

Inhedler, Barbel. & Piaget, Jean. *The Growth of Logical Thinking From Childhood to Adolescence.* New York: Basic Books, 1958.

Joseph, Stephen. & Linley, P. Alex. "Positive Adjustment To Threatening Events: An Orgasmic Valuing Theory Of Growth Through Adversity." *Review Of General Psychology,* 9. 2005. 262-280.

Kail Robert. & Cavanaugh John C. *Human Development: A Life-Span View.* Cengage Learning, 6th ed. 2012.

Kain, Philip J. *Hegel and The Other.* Albany: State University of New York Press, 2005.

Kaplan, Helen S. "Intimacy Disorders And Sexual Panic States." *Journal of Sex and Marital Therapy.* 14 (1). 1988. 3-12.

Kasser, Tim. & Sheldon, Ken M. "Non-becoming, Alienated Becoming, and Authentic Becoming: A Goal Based Approach." In J. Greenberg, S. L. Koole & T. Pyszczynsk (Eds.). *Handbook of Experimental Existential Psychology.* New York: Guilford Press, 2004. 486-499.

Kopp, Sheldon. *If You Meet The Buddha On The Road, Kill Him.* New York: Bantam Books, 1982.

References

Kopp, Sheldon. *Rock, Paper, Scissors*. Minnesota: Company Care Publisher, 1989.

Kottler, Jeffery A. 2010. *On Being A Therapist* (4th edition). New York: Jossey-Bass.

Kubler-Ross, Elizabeth. *On Death And Dying*. New York: Scribner, 1977.

Laing, Ronald D. *The Divided Self: An Existential Study In Sanity And Madness*. Harmondsworth: Penguin, 1965.

Laing, Ronald D. *Wisdom, Madness And Folly: The Making Of A Psychiatrist 1927-1957*. London: Macmillan, 1985.

Maslow, Abraham H. *Towards a Psychology Of Being* (2nd edition). New York: D. Van Nostrand, 1968.

Maslow, Abraham H.. *The Further Reaches of Human Nature*. New York: Penguin, 1971.

May, Rollo. *Love and Will*. New York: Norton Press, 1969.

May, Rollo. *The Courage to Create*. New York: Norton Press, 1976.

Millon, Theodore. *Personality Disorders in Modern Life* (2nd edition). New York: Wiley, 2004.

Minuchin, Salvador. *Family Therapy Techniques*. Boston: Harvard University Press, 1981.

Mitchell, Juliet. 2003. Siblings: Sex And Violence. New York: Basic Books.

Mitchell, Juliet. *Mad Men and Medusas*. New York: Basic Books, 2001.

Montuori, Alfanso & Fahim, Urusa. "Cross-Cultural Encounter as an Opportunity for Personal Growth." *Journal of Humanistic Psychology*, 44. 2004. 243-265.

Moody, Harry R. *Aging: Concepts and Controversies*. (8th edition). California: Sage Publications, 2014.

Napir, Augustas & Whitaker, Carl. *The Family Crucible: The Intense Experience of Family Therapy*. New York: Harper & Row, 1988.

Pearce, W. Barnett. Making Social Worlds: A Communication Perspective. Malden, MA: Blackwell, 2007.

Pearson, Carol S. *Awakening the Heroes Within*. New York: Harper Collins Publishers, 1991.

Perls, Fitz S. *Gestalt Therapy Verbatim*. California: Real People Press, 1969.

Ridley, Charles R. *Overcoming Unintentional Racism in Counseling and Therapy: A Practitioner's Guide to Intentional Interventions* (2nd edition). California: Sage Publications, 2005.

Rogers, Carl. *On Becoming a Person: A Therapist View Of Psychotherapy*. Massachusetts: Houghton Mifflin, 1961.

Russell, Robert & Laing, Ronald D. *R.D. Laing And Me, Lessons In Love*. New York: Hillgarth Press, 1992.

Sacco, P.A. & Laino, Debra. *Madonna Complex*. California: Chipmunka Publishing, 2011.

Satir, Virginia. *Conjoint Family Therapy*. CA: Science and Behavior Books, 1983.

Satir, Virginia. *The New People Making*. CA: Science and Behavior Books, 1988.

References

Satir, Virginia. *Your Many Faces* (3rd revised edition). New York: Celestial Arts, 2009.

Schneider, Kirk J. *Existential-Integrative Psychotherapy.* New York: Routledge, 2008.

Schwitzer, Allen M. "Diagnosing, Conceptualizing, And Treating Eating Disorders Not Otherwise Specified: A Comprehensive Practice Model." *Journal of Counseling and Development*, 90 (3). 2012. 281-9.

Shaffer, David R. & Kipp, Kathrine. *Developmental Psychology: Childhood and Adolescence.* Cengage Learning: 9th ed. 2013.

Sheldon, Ken M. & Kasser, Tim. "Coherence and Congruence: Two Aspects of Personality Integration." *Journal of Personality & Social Psychology*, 68. 1995. 531-543.

Sheldon, Ken M. & Kasser, Tim. "Getting Older, Getting Better: Personal Strivings and Psychological Maturity Across The Life Span." *Developmental Psychology*, 37. 2001. 495-501.

Sieglelman, Ellen. *Metaphor and Meaning In Psychotherapy.* New York: Guilford Press, 1990.

Sleeth, Daniel B. "Integral Love: The Role of Love in Clinical Practice as a Rite of Passage". *Journal of Humanistic Psychology*, 50. 2010. 471-494.

Spade, Joan. *The Kaleidoscope of Gender.* London: Sage Publication, 2013.

Speyner, John A. *The Madonna/Whore Complex: A Primal Theory Interpretation.* The Primal Psychotherapy Page. primal-page.com, 2011.

Stein, Robert. *Betrayal of Soul In Psychotherapy*. New York: Spring Publications, 1998.

Stein, Robert. *Incest and Human Love*. New York: Spring Publications, 1998.

Sullivan, Harry S. *The Interpersonal Theory of Psychiatry*. New York: Norton & Co., 1953.

Sullivan, Harry S. *The Fusion of Psychiatry And Social Science*. New York: Norton & Co., 1964.

Weisz, John R. *Psychotherapy For Children and Adolescents: Evidence-Based Treatment and Case Examples*. Cambridge University Press, 2004.

William, Paris. *Rethinking Madness: Towards A Paradigm Shift In Our Understanding And Treatment Of Psychosis*. California: Sky's Edge, 2012.

Whitaker, Carl. & Bumberry, William M. *Dancing With The Family: A Symbolic Experiential Approach*. New York: Brunner/Mazel, 1988.

Whitaker, C. & Malone, Thomas. *The Roots Of Psychotherapy*. New York: Routledge Publishers, 1993.

Whitaker, Carl. & Malone, Thomas. *The Involvement Of The Professional Therapist*. w.w.w.all-aboutpsychology.com, 2011.

Wolf, Naomi. *Promiscuities: A Secret History of Female Desire*. London: Chatto and Windus, 1997.

Ungar, Michael. *Strength-Based Counseling With At-Risk Youth*. (2nd ed.). California: Sage Publications, 2006.

Yalom, Irwin D. *Existential Psychotherapy*. New York: Basic Books, 1980.

References

Yalom, Irwin D. *The Theory And Practice Of Group Psychotherapy* (5th edition). New York: Basic Books, 2005.

Yalom, Irwin D. *Love's Executioner And Other Tales Of Psychotherapy*. New York: Basic Books, 2012.

Veis Djalali

ଔଔଔଔଔଔଔଔ

www.ingramcontent.com/pod-product-compliance
Lightning Source LLC
Chambersburg PA
CBHW070554270326
41926CB00013B/2304